FIELD NOTES

Volume 1

By Angela Sheldrick

PHOTOGRAPHY
Mia Collis
Robert Carr-Hartley
Roan Carr-Hartley
Francisco Grimaldi
Neville Sheldrick

COMPILED BY
Sean Michael

DESIGNED BY
Angela Sheldrick

“Elephant conservation is not the work of a moment, but a monumental, multi-generational commitment.”

Angela Sheldrick

TABLE OF CONTENTS

INTRODUCTION

By Angela Sheldrick

I have been lucky to live a lifetime in Kenya's wild spaces. My childhood played out in the red earth of Tsavo and later beneath the leafy croton trees of Nairobi National Park. As I grew up around a motley crew of baby rhinos, elephants, zebras, and antelope — just to name a few — so many monumental things were unfolding around me.

My father, David Sheldrick, was the founding warden of Tsavo East National Park. Every night around the dinner table, he would regale us with spellbinding tales of the day's events: ambushing poachers, charging elephants, raging rivers, daring rescues. Meanwhile, my mother, Daphne Sheldrick, was working around the clock raising orphaned elephants and rhinos, all the while trying to crack the code of how to raise the infant elephant babies. I have such a crystallised memory of her mixing milk, with a little elephant trunk twirled around her wrist.

These were the scenes that narrated my own upbringing. The Sheldrick Wildlife Trust has grown over the decades, evolving into a multi-faceted organisation spanning elephant and rhino conservation, habitat preservation, anti-poaching, aerial operations, field veterinary, and community outreach. What began as a single stable has morphed into a world-renowned Orphans' Project that has successfully raised more than 300 orphaned elephants. As we raise the orphans of today, our pilots, rangers, vet units, and field teams are working hard to ensure they always have wild spaces to call home.

But as much as things have changed, so much remains exactly the same. My husband, Robert, and I have raised our sons in the same great wildernesses that shaped my life. Mirroring my own childhood, we still gather around the dinner table every night to regale each other with the day's stories. These, too, mirror the stories I grew up with: orphaned elephants rescued, poachers apprehended, wild lives saved.

A lifetime of conversations around the dinner table are what inspired me to start writing Field Notes in 2019. I realised there were so many as-yet-untold stories — little-known sides of our conservation work, incredible tales from the field, insights into the landscapes in which we work and the species we protect, tales of Kenya's history and ecology and environment. We settled on "Field Notes", a monthly email newsletter in which I could share my stories — our stories — with an audience beyond the dinner table.

Five years into Field Notes, Volume I is a compilation of my favourite stories. I hope you enjoy reading them as much as I enjoyed telling them.

THE POWER OF LOVE

— November 2023 —

"Just like a human child, a baby elephant captures your heart entirely – so utterly dependent and incredibly intelligent. Although a baby elephant duplicates humans in terms of age, they are certainly much more advanced than the human equivalent in early infancy and much more responsible and wiser in childhood and adolescence."

– Daphne Sheldrick -

As someone who had the unique experience of growing up with orphaned elephants as my peers, then raising them alongside my own children, I can attest to the truth of Daphne's words. Elephants are indeed strikingly similar to ourselves. Like us, they have distinct and dynamic personalities. They feel emotions deeply and have clever, capable brains that are always whirring. Each one is completely unique and utterly enchanting.

Through this lens, one must marvel at my mother's perseverance. The early days, first in Tsavo and later in Nairobi, were an era of trial and error. No one had yet successfully raised an orphaned infant African elephant. Daphne and David endured a steady stream of heartbreak, as they discovered just how complex and sensitive these little creatures are. While orphans rescued at an older age thrived, infants remained a cipher that seemed impossible to decode.

Developing the proper milk formula of an infant orphan elephant was a journey of its own… but that is a story for another day. Of equal — or, I would argue, greater — importance was understanding the husbandry needed to successfully help these young elephants navigate the darkest chapter of their lives.

Of course, we wouldn't call any of these early cases a complete loss. Rather, they paved the way for all the orphans who would follow in their footsteps. Daphne realised that infant orphaned elephants didn't just need the essentials. Shelter, sustenance, veterinary care — all these things were vital, but their psychological well-being hinged on much deeper, more nuanced care. A telling anecdote about Olmeg, the very first orphaned elephant Daphne raised at our Nairobi Nursery, illustrates this:

There was nothing for it but to relegate Baron the rooster and his wives to a box in the kitchen, so that Olmeg could occupy the chicken house. This was a disaster — Olmeg bellowed constantly, clearly feeling claustrophobic, until we could stand it no longer and had to let him out. We tried exercising him around the car park for half an hour or so at a time in order to tire him out, but this didn't work either, for whenever we put him back the bellowing began all over again, added to which he clearly enjoyed the nocturnal outings.

In the end, Jill [my older sister] suggested Olmeg share her bedroom, despite the fact that he was still producing extremely smelly, watery stools. We replaced the carpet on her bedroom floor with a bed of hay and here the little elephant eventually settled down to sleep, after several attempts to climb onto Jill's bed.

As a steady succession of new rescues came into our care, it also became clear that raising infant orphaned elephants wasn't a one-woman job. It was critical that orphans didn't become overly dependent on any single individual — and equally, the task was too great for one person to shoulder alone. As our orphan herd grew, the role of Keepers became increasingly important. Today, we have more than 50 Keepers working across our five orphan units.

Safari

Instead of recruiting Keepers from one specific tribe or locality, we hire from across Kenya. Our logic is that each person, with their diverse background, opens a whole new dimension to the role. This strategy has the added bonus of fostering conservation awareness across the country. Keepers become vital ambassadors within their own communities. Over the years, many orphans have been saved by ordinary people who developed empathy for elephants through a Keeper who is a father, uncle, friend, or neighbour.

People are always curious what qualifications we look for in a Keeper. It's not anything one would find on a resumé. While many of our Keepers have shambas or raise livestock back home, none have worked professionally with elephants before. However, all experiences and qualifications melt away when confronted with our orphan herd. Elephants have a way of distilling a person to their purest form. Our orphans are quick to identify the 'X factor' that makes an excellent Keeper, which is why we ultimately put recruitment in their capable hands. New candidates join the orphan herd on a trial basis, and if they are embraced by the elephants, they are hired as a full-time Keeper.

We call it the 'X factor,' but to assign an all-encompassing human trait, it would be empathy. People who succeed with orphaned elephants are pure of heart, graced with a quiet confidence and unfaltering dedication.

People who possess these qualities are one in a million — yet, miraculously, they continue to find their way into our orbit, usually through the most unexpected routes. Misheck, who has been with us for more than three decades, has a mystical ability to convince orphans who have all but given up to return to the land of the living. He was a night watchman before we hired him — and from these humble beginnings, one of our most gifted Keepers emerged.

Peter, another of our longest serving Keepers, was employed as a construction worker in Nairobi when he was introduced to the Trust. He became enchanted by the baby elephants and applied for the role. He is an incredibly talented Keeper who has been on almost all our orphan rescues. Joseph, a rising star on our team, started as an anti-poaching ranger. Now, he is taking on some of our most challenging orphan cases. These men are just three among many, many examples of extraordinary talent on our team.

Keepers play the role of caregiver and healer. As Daphne recognised all those years ago, an orphan's psychological state is even more important than any physical injuries they must overcome. It is essential to have a comprehensive understanding of their rescue story, as this helps unlock what they need to move forward.

Orphans who experienced pain and suffering often exhibit behaviour that mirrors post-traumatic stress syndrome in humans. Healing the psychological effects of such stress is imperative — and no small task. It takes time, patience, and the all-important empathy. Some orphans accept their new family from the outset, others take weeks before beginning to thaw, still others always remain a bit standoffish. We are there to help every orphan overcome their personal traumas, without trying to reshape their personalities.

Given this weighty undertaking, one might mistakenly assume that our Nurseries are rather sombre places. That couldn't be further from the truth. Our goal is to create a joy-filled cocoon for each orphan — a secure, stress-free environment where they feel loved, supported, and safe.

This strategy, in its beautiful simplicity, is transformative. There is nothing better than witnessing an orphan who arrives furtive and withdrawn begin to shed their shell. It's a transformation that begins within, but spreads outwardly: dull eyes begin to sparkle, once-limp ears extend like butterfly wings, frightened mock-charges give way to a trunk tentatively extended in greeting.

I often reflect upon the metamorphosis of Kerrio, who came to us physically paralysed and physiologically damaged. Day and night, her Keepers painstakingly earned her trust. With this trust came transformation. As Kerrio's mental state improved, her strength returned. The little elephant who we thought might never walk properly again came back to life. A few laboured steps gave way to short forays around the compound, then longer journeys to join the rest of the orphans. Now Kerrio is the matriarch of our Nursery herd — a remarkable female with an enormous capacity to love, for both her orphan 'kids' and her Keeper 'parents'.

There are so many stories like Kerrio's unfolding, across all our orphan units. The common thread — the secret ingredient, if you will — that carries them through their darkest days, helping them blossom into happy, well-adjusted elephants, is love.

As my mother used to say, animals weave their way into one's heart so completely. It is only fitting, then, that we raise them with our whole hearts. This emotional investment is reciprocated — for the love of an elephant lasts a lifetime. I am reminded of this every time an ex-orphan returns 'home' to proudly debut their newly born baby to the men who raised her.

When you have earned the love of an elephant, they too keep you in their hearts forever.

THE NAIROBI NURSERY, A PLACE OF BEGINNINGS

— January 2024 —

Long before the sun's first rays have greeted the horizon, the Nairobi Nursery is already whirring with activity. Clinks and clanks emerge from the milk mixing areas, as Keepers carefully measure out the formulas for the morning's first bottle feed. A crackling fire is lit in the canteen, from which the smell of chapatis and freshly brewed chai wafts across the compound.

The orphans typically wake up in a domino effect. Drowsy rumbles escalate into a chorus of chatter, as the orphans rise, one after the other, and catch up with their neighbours after a night's separation. Some of the more impatient babies trundle over to the bunk in the corner of their bedroom, reaching their trunk to unceremoniously tug the blanket off their Keeper. Others sleep on, relishing every last minute of shut-eye.

Like magic, two bottles are delivered outside each orphan's stable or stockade promptly at 6 o'clock. Once everyone's belly is full, the day can officially begin. The youngest elephants are the first to emerge from their stables. Swaddled in their colourful blankets, which ward off the morning chill, they relish this brief time in which they rule the Nursery. Some saunter over to say hello to Maxwell the rhino, while others browse on every errant shrub and branch with great importance.

The pint-sized reign is broken as the rest of the orphan herd is let out of their stables. The mini matriarchs cluster around the blanket babies, while the junior bulls swagger around with great importance. Mzinga, our resident rhino whisperer, can usually be found at Maxwell's gate, caressing the rhino with her trunk. Shujaa, who can never resist an opportunity to go off-piste, trundles atop the visitor platform so he can access the untapped bounties of greens.

Raha the black rhino operates on her own schedule. She enjoys a later lie-in, resting until the sun has fully revealed itself. Clad in her own thick blanket, she follows her Keepers into the forest, usually accompanied by an animated series of squeaks and snorts. Rhinos are a solitary species, so Raha follows her own beat during the day. Rhinos can also be quite ornery, so her Keepers' best-laid plans are often waylaid by the headstrong young girl!

The orphans' waking hours are spent exploring Nairobi National Park. No two days are alike, which is only fitting for a highly intelligent species that thrives off constant stimulation. Typically, the Keepers suggest a direction, guiding the herd towards a new freshwater mud wallow or a verdant patch of greens.

These adventures proceed, rain or shine. The Keepers are fully kitted out for any sort of weather, while the orphans, being wild animals, must get used to all nature's whims. The youngest orphans are girded against the elements in their blankets, and on very rainy days, they remain in the shelter of their stables until the skies clear up. (Meanwhile, in particularly inclement weather, some enterprising older orphans try to work their way beneath a Keeper's umbrella!)

As the orphans embark upon their day, the rest of the compound also comes to life. The Nairobi Nursery serves as the headquarters for all our northern units. The on-site workshop manages vehicle maintenance and fabrication for our teams, from Meru to Mount Kenya to the Rift Valley. The whir of welders and hum of engines fills the air, as the team conducts repairs and upgrades.

The orphans receive their 9 o'clock milk feed in the forest, while the 11 o'clock meal unfolds down at the mud bath. This coincides with our daily public visit, in which guests are invited to observe the orphans during their midday meal and mud bath. Nursery Head Keeper Edwin or his deputy narrates the hour, providing context about each orphan's rescue story and an overview of our work in the field. It is one of our greatest privileges to welcome people from all over the world to the Nursery, meeting donors and spreading our conservation mission.

During the Nursery stage, most orphans are fed two bottles of milk, every three hours, while the youngest are fed on-demand. Each baby enjoys a specific formula that is tailored to their age and nutritional needs. Milk mixing is a 24-hour role, rotated between the Keepers, in order to ensure that every feeding unfolds like clockwork. The orphans are taskmasters in this department: They are prompt timekeepers and know exactly when the next feeding is due. If milk bottles arrive even a minute late, they are quick to lodge their complaints!

For every milk feed, the orphans are brought down in small groups. These are usually organised by age, although some special cases earn themselves a place in a different group. (Muridjo, our fabulously contrarian girl, springs to mind — she started bullying her peers during milk feeds, so she was upgraded to an older group, who semi-effectively keep her in line.)

The elephants dash as fast as their stout legs will carry them, propelled by the promise of milk. The more resourceful individuals are quick to orchestrate milk heists, either targeting the wheelbarrow that holds all the empty bottles or honing in on a smaller orphan who has yet to finish their share. The Keepers must be on high alert in order to thwart their machinations!

During the dry season, the orphans can rely on the mud bath outside Daphne's house for all their wallowing. But the rains bring about all manner of impromptu delights, as puddles, mud slicks, and pools spring up throughout the forest. Some orphans reliably dive headfirst into any body of water, while others prefer a dainty soil dusting on the edges. Often, it is the bulls with the greatest bravado who are most hesitant — it never ceases to entertain, watching the big elephants steel themselves on the edge of the smallest pools, waiting determinedly for their friends to enter uncharted waters first.

People always marvel at the tidiness of our compounds. This is a top priority — but keeping everything shipshape takes a lot of effort. While one team of Keepers chaperones the orphans in the forest, another cleans the stables and stockades, cuts greens, washes blankets, and otherwise ensures everything is in order. Our groundskeepers — some of whom have been in the Trust's employ from the very beginning — meticulously tend to the Nursery's gardens and grounds. They know every shrub, flower, tree, and plant by heart.

While Nairobi National Park is perhaps best known for its acacia-dotted plains, set against the distant backdrop of the Nairobi skyline, the Nursery sits within a forested corner of the park. During the rainy season, as is the case right now, the undergrowth can become quite thick. The Keepers must be vigilant about monitoring their little charges, as they share the park with lions, hyenas, leopards, and jackals. Ironically, it is often the most innocuous interlopers who create the biggest drama — the surprise appearance of a chameleon or a tortoise can send the entire orphan herd into a panic!

Whatever adventures the day might bring, our Keepers are there to document it all. Armed with their phones, cameras, and old-fashioned journals, they video, photograph, and diarise the happenings, from sunup to sundown. At the end of each month, this content — from across all five orphan units — is collated into an update to share with our global family of foster parents. We have decades of daily Keepers' Diaries. Through this historic catalogue of our orphans' stories, we also have a uniquely in-depth and intimate perspective into elephant behaviour.

Come 5 o'clock, the entire compound starts to wind down. While the hum of the workshop lulls, sizzles and snaps can be heard from the canteen, where the cook is preparing dinner for the staff. Meanwhile, the Keepers have been hard at work ensuring the orphans' bedrooms are ready for bedtime. Every stable and stockade has been stripped and lined with a puffy layer of hay. They are stocked with bundles of freshly cut greens, which the orphans snack on throughout the night, and two bottles of milk wait outside each gate for the evening feed. Maxwell enjoys a bedtime treat of sliced pineapples, bananas, and watermelon, while Raha chomps in a circular fashion around her suspended bundles of greens.

Orphans know which bedroom is theirs and feel quite attached to it. (I will never forget the outrage of Bondeni, Kindani, and Kinyei when we dared to change their Nursery rooming arrangements!) The youngest babies tend to approach bedtime with great gusto. They dash home in a frenzy of flapping ears, pumping legs, and flailing trunks, making a beeline for their stables. When they outgrow their fragile infancy, orphans are moved into open-air stockades, which offer a touch more space and independence.

As the day draws to a close, the night is just beginning for our next shift. At the Nursery, each orphan is roomed with a dedicated Keeper, who provides care, company, and milk feedings through the night. This role requires vigilance, as the orphans must be carefully monitored during their fragile infancy. The rainy season has been a rather sleepless time for the poor night shift, as their little charges protest the sound of thunder and rain battering the stable roofs.

Raising an orphaned elephant is not the work of a few years, but the commitment of a lifetime. An orphan may remain in our care for upwards of a decade until they feel ready to reclaim their place in the wild, and even then, our field teams continue to look after them. In the wider narrative of an orphan's life, the Nursery is but a brief stage. But there is something very special about the place where it all begins.

As I write this, our current herd of Nursery orphans are tucked into their bedrooms. In time, these little elephants will be giants of Tsavo, spending their night under the star-spangled skies of Kenya's greatest wilderness. But for now, their full bellies rise and fall in tune with the nocturnal noises of Nairobi National Park beyond, watched over by their surrogate family.

TSAVO, A LAND WHERE TIME DOESN'T COUNT

— May 2020 —

Tsavo is one of those rare gems where nature still reigns. That fact is profoundly evident in years when we are graced with long rains. Life abounds: Birds chirp from every branch and ipomea creepers blanket every surface, creating a white veil of flowers atop all the greenery. Staring across its vast horizon, where the heavens dip to meet the land, one can't help but think this is the world as it should be.

David and Daphne Sheldrick dedicated their lives to creating a National Park out of this extraordinary land, and it is the place I have been fortunate enough to call home since birth. Tsavo has a magic that is difficult to put into words, but no one could describe it better than my mother. Daphne's absolute love for Tsavo can be felt profoundly through her writing:

"Tsavo is a land where time doesn't count and where everything is just as it was long ago. Trees and flowers are left to grow unchecked, and streams and rivers flow where they will. Cotton wool clouds drift across a sky of brilliant blue whose clarity is unsullied by pollution. Here, all creatures live in accordance with a law that has governed nature since the world was new the survival of the fittest. We, who lead sheltered and protected lives, might think of it as a cruel and rather frightening place, for it is a pristine world where mercy is unknown, but it is intensely fascinating with a mysterious charm of its very own that is pure and beautiful.

Those that have once tasted its enchantment find it addictive and can never again escape its spell. They are drawn back as though by a magnet to savour the solace that it imparts to the soul. There, stepping back in time, we glimpse the world of yesterday, and we will be reminded that we share it with many other creatures who are also a part of creation with a specific purpose to their being, a vital link in the chain of life. Then thinking of the wonders all around us, we become mindful also of a great responsibility that has been vested in us, the responsibility to keep the chain of life intact, for to break a link is to jeopardise our own survival and that of many other creatures too. Suddenly things fall into place and we begin to understand a little more about living, and a little more about ourselves as well which is the key to being at peace with oneself and with others.

The solitude of a wild place fulfils another important function in a busy world, for it stirs the chords of our being and appeases a basic yearning deep inside ourselves for things we have probably never known and cannot begin to understand. But here, people caught up in the bustle of life can escape and find themselves afresh in a primitive place where all other cares fade before the basic one of survival."

Our conservation story began in 1948, when Tsavo was set aside for all things wild. David, who was appointed its founding warden, was given the daunting task of transforming this vast expanse into a place where wildlife could thrive. He and his team were confronted with a largely dense thicket, home to elephants scarred by years of being poached and lions with man-eating tendencies.

For the next three decades, they navigated droughts and floods, tackled poaching and political threats, and turned Tsavo into the model for conservation that it is today. (If one ever doubts their commitment to the cause, we need only remember the three-month stint David and his workforce spent marooned on the north bank of the Athi River, after extensive floods left them well and truly stranded! Rather than despair, they devised a way to have supplies ferried across in a small rubber dinghy attached to a cable spanning the raging torrents, so they could continue their work unabated.)

Rivers give and rivers take — and they certainly present their fair share of challenges. One of David's earliest achievements was finding a way to cross the Galana River to unlock the 3,000 square miles of Tsavo that lay beyond its northern bank. It took over a year to complete, but the Lugard's Causeway was an extraordinary accomplishment, as they successfully diverted the Galana River and connected the park from top to bottom. This was a practical undertaking, but also something more visionary: After spanning the Galana, the roads follow elephant trails through the Mpia Gap and into the wilds of the north, a place dominated by magnificent tuskers and giant baobab trees. David saw the potential in this remarkable corner of Tsavo, and it is no coincidence that it is where Ithumba, one of our three Reintegration Units, now sits.

In a place as arid as Tsavo, rivers become the focal point. Its perennial Tsavo and Athi/Galana Rivers are certainly the places where all life converges, while the seasonal Tiva River to the north and Voi River to the south have their own share of action. Tall acacia, newtonia, and tamarind trees fringe the rivers and tributaries, along with my favourite, the doum palms. It was in the shade of these palms that we would set up camp during my childhood. David was very particular in this regard, and always picked a site that was comfortable, and his safaris were well-organised, and situated in a picturesque area. I have many fond memories of these impeccable camps, basking in nature and watching the sun glimmer above the hulking Yatta Plateau.

For if there is one landmark inextricably linked to Tsavo, it is the Yatta Plateau. This feat of nature dominates the horizon beginning in Ol Donyo Sabuk, close to Nairobi, and continues south through the Park for nearly 300 kilometres. It serves as the main watershed for the Athi and Galana Rivers and their tributaries. Springs bubble from its steep escarpments, shaded by giant fig trees clinging onto granite boulders. These springs are a source of life during the dry season, which in turn makes them vulnerable to poachers. It was David who recruited Tsavo's first anti-poaching force, and following his blueprint, our field teams continue to place special focus on these vulnerable and precious areas.

Protecting all of Tsavo's wild residents is no small task: The park is home to more than 70 mammal species, along with some 500 types of birds. Kenya's most iconic species — elephants, buffalos, rhinos, giraffes, and lions — preside over its plains. These are the sights that game drives are made of, but I am equally captivated by all that is hidden from our eyes. Take, for instance, the naked mole rat, which leads its life entirely underground. The next time you look upon the Yatta Plateau, just imagine these burrowing machines within, feasting on tubers and creating vast labyrinths amidst the lava. Tsavo is inhabited by the big and the small, each as fascinating as the next, and it needs many lifetimes to unearth and fully understand all its fascinating wonders.

Tsavo has defined my life. While David was creating a network of roads snaking 2,000 kilometres through the park, I was taking my first steps in its red earth. While Daphne was hand-raising orphaned elephants and rhinos, I was enjoying my bottle right alongside them. It is ironic that the campsite along the banks of the Galana River, where I have so many fond childhood memories with my parents, is now the very place where the Sheldrick Wildlife Trust owns an Eco Lodge called Galdessa. Here, we invite guests to unlock the secrets of Tsavo for themselves, to immerse themselves in its wonders and enjoy exclusive access to the property. By staying at Galdessa, you also directly contribute to the continued protection of Tsavo, as all proceeds from our Eco Lodges are reinvested into our conservation projects.

This template is especially fitting now, at a time when we need food for the soul more than ever. I always go back to Daphne's quote: "The solitude of a wild place fulfils another important function in a busy world, for it stirs the chords of our being and appeases a basic yearning deep inside ourselves for things we have probably never known and cannot begin to understand."

Tsavo, in all its mystery and wonder, has the power to enchant us in a way that we didn't even know was possible in today's modern world. When you allow yourself to be cast under its spell, you too will find yourself transported on a beautiful journey of self-discovery.

THE MAKINGS OF A MATRIARCH

— April 2020 —

My father, David Sheldrick, said it best: "The more one knows about animals, the more one realises how much we still have to learn."

I have spent my entire life around elephants, yet they continue to astonish me in the very best way. One might think that, after working long days and sleepless nights by their little charges' sides, our Keepers — many of whom have been with us for decades — might have also discovered all the secrets that elephants hold within them, but that is not the case. We have witnessed the orphans we have raised from infancy behave in remarkable ways and accomplish extraordinary feats. Put simply, they never cease to amaze us.

Over 160 of our orphaned elephants are now living wild, many with their own babies by their sides. Each one has a story of survival that began on the fateful day that left them orphaned. They come from all over the country, separated from their biological families in devastating circumstances. Directly or indirectly, most of our elephants were orphaned at the hands of humans. Their trauma is often both physical and psychological, as elephants are deeply feeling creatures and don't soon forget the families they lost. And yet, all our orphans have opened their hearts to both their human Keepers and fellow elephant orphans, forming tight familial bonds that last a lifetime.

The success behind our orphans is undoubtedly due to the determination and courage of one woman. Raising an orphaned elephant is a long and often very fraught journey. Nature has made infant elephants more fragile than most, and it took many years of trial and error for my mother, Dame Daphne Sheldrick, to crack the code.

Helping these young elephants navigate their formative, milk-dependent years was the first challenge. Then she was confronted with the next, monumental obstacle: How could we return these elephants to the wild where they rightfully belong, mindful that in order for them to be fully accepted by the wild community, they needed to be emotionally stable and well-versed in the natural ways of elephants? We could do our best to love and nurture these highly intelligent creatures when they were babies, but their transition to the wild presented a whole new set of challenges that could not be taught by any human.

Of course, Daphne was never daunted by a challenge. She understood that an elephant's life mirrors our own, but these were lessons that she could not impart herself. The orphans needed to learn elephant ways from their own kind.

And that is where the next miracle in a series of universal marvels stepped in, in the form of Eleanor. Born in 1959, she was orphaned — likely at the hands of poachers — before her second birthday, which is when she entered our lives. Simply put, Eleanor was a god-send. It was as if she knew Daphne needed her help for this next phase. Instead of going wild with the orphans Samson and Fatuma, she chose to remain with us for many years once she was grown. It was as if her motherly instincts kept her by Daphne's side, and she served as a crucial mentor who paved the way for other orphans to follow.

Eleanor eventually heard the call of the wild, but not before making an indelible impact on our Orphans' Project. Helping other elephants through that transitory stage could not have happened without her initial help. Ever since, we have been blessed with a rota of remarkable females who have stepped up and served as mentors to the orphans who are following in their footsteps. Even when they are toddling around the Nursery, certain females feel the instinct to take over where their human family cannot possibly fill the void.

In the wild, baby elephants are raised in a cocoon of love. Mothers and nannies wrap their trunks around a calf's belly, over its shoulder, under its neck, often touching its mouth. It's a beautiful, joyful, communal affair — and these are all behaviours we also observe from the more maternal members of our orphan herd. It's as if they know that younger orphans thrive on tactile affection, and they provide it in abundance.

Behind every successful elephant dynasty, you will find a wise matriarch who carries a treasure trove of knowledge. They have a unique influence over group decision-making, and, like our own leaders, the most successful may even possess certain personality traits. This is very much the case for wild elephant herds, but how could we account for the way in which our orphans form their own herds and not only survive, but truly thrive?

Seeing our ex-orphan herds blossom under the leadership of a chosen older female, be it Yatta or Emily or Mbegu, we cannot help but wonder, 'what are the makings of a matriarch?' How do our orphans select their chosen leader when it is not genetically ingrained, and what defines her? The selection of our ex-orphans' elder stateswomen seems to naturally unfold, but we have found that it is usually one of those doting female figures who emerged during the Nursery stage, and who seems to possess those crucial leadership qualities from the outset. Perhaps it is in their genes, or perhaps it is formulated over years of cultivating a compassionate 'personality' (to assign them that anthropomorphic quality) towards other elephants.

In the face of natural adversity, our ex-orphans show their true mettle. When a brutal drought gripped much of Kenya in 2017, elephants struggled enormously. We worried about how our ex-orphans would fare, but we needn't have: Emily and her ex-orphan herd made for the ranch-lands adjacent to Tsavo East National Park, which still had ample vegetation to sustain them until the rains broke many months later. This was a journey of over 100 kilometres each way, but all the members of Emily's herd persevered — with Ndara's newborn baby, Neptune, underfoot no less! When they showed up at our Voi stockades later that year, they were in remarkably good health and spirits.

We cannot underscore what a monumental achievement this was. Emily was just 24 years old at the time. She was also orphaned as an infant, and thus never had the opportunity to inherit wisdom from older family members. Despite this, she managed to negotiate a dry season which tragically claimed the lives of over 400 elephants in just a few months, succeeding where much more experienced individuals were not so lucky. We could not help but marvel at the intuitiveness of our ex-orphans and Emily's ability to lead and make those crucial decisions, which at the end of the day can mean life or death for a herd.

It is not unusual for our orphans to be in the company of wild friends. In the green seasons, Emily and her herd of independent orphans can be found absorbed within the ranks of huge aggregations of elephants, wild herds numbering close to 800 individuals. Over the years, our ex-orphans and matriarchs have developed these crucial close relationships with wild friends — and these friendships play a key role in how our orphans learn the ropes as they navigate Tsavo's vast landscape.

It is important to remember that our ex-orphan herds are not of a natural composition. They are not composed of an elder, mothers, aunts, sisters, and babies. Instead, they are led by an elected matriarch, chosen based on her leadership qualities and personality, and 'adopted' sisters of a similar age. Eventually, their herds get bigger, as they successfully mate and have their own wild-born babies tottering about their feet.

While their transition to the wild is seamless, our ex-orphans never forget their origins: Just as Eleanor did all those years ago, they come back to mentor the younger orphans. When it is time to help them make the transition towards a more independent life, it is our ex-orphans who perform the all-important task of taking their younger counterparts under their wings, providing the bridging oversight as they fraternise with wild herds.

We are very excited about what the future holds for our many matriarchs in the making. Every day, we witness remarkable stories unfolding across all our units. At Umani Springs, Lima Lima has stepped up as a proxy matriarch, exacting the wishes of Murera, who is the herd's older, physically compromised matriarch. Ever since her earliest days at the Nursery, Mbegu has been a force to be reckoned with, and even as one of the youngest members of the Voi herd, she immediately emerged as a clear leader. In Ithumba, females like Olare, Loijuk, and Mutara continue to show their leadership acumen.

While a tragic twist of fate left each of these elephants orphaned, they persevered and emerged as extraordinarily capable matriarchs with all the natural skills and wisdom required. That, to me, is the greatest miracle of all.

WINGS FOR WILDLIFE

— September 2021 —

The sounds of a Super Cub flying low and slow — to me, these are the sounds of conservation at work. My father, David Sheldrick, was an early proponent of using aircraft for conservation. His wings of choice came in the form of the Super Cub, a versatile plane that is perfectly at home patrolling the bush.

David was famously adept at landing it in remarkably difficult conditions, often on dusty tracks or river sandbanks to meet with his teams in situ. I remember him flying on patrol, slowing the Super Cub to a near-hover to communicate with his rangers on the ground, no different than as if he was talking to them from the driver's seat of a Land Cruiser! This showed that, in the hands of an experienced pilot, there is little the Super Cub cannot do. It is certainly the ideal tool for a National Park the size of Tsavo. As a child, I spent endless happy hours on Tsavo's dusty airstrips, waiting for my father's return and longing for all the stories from the day — because in Tsavo, no day is ever dull.

And so, it was only fitting that a Super Cub would serve as the inaugural aircraft in our fleet, launching the Trust's Aerial Surveillance Unit in 2008. I can honestly say that this was the single greatest turning point in our operations, quite literally elevating our capabilities for conservation. Suddenly, we had all of Tsavo not only within our view, but also within our reach. Aircraft enhance our work in the most perfect way, complementing the forensic approach of our ground teams with broader capabilities that can only be achieved in the sky. Pilots can cover an area in a fraction of time that it would take on the ground. Crucially, they can also land in areas that are inaccessible for vehicles — of which there are many in this wild landscape.

It has been more than a decade since we got our first Super Cub. Our fleet has expanded to fixed-wing airplanes and helicopters, each of which plays a unique supporting role in our work. One of our newest additions, a Baby Caravan STW, is already proving its mettle. As our largest airplane yet, it can safely fly in most weather conditions, undertake night operations, and has the capacity to carry up to ten passengers — or a large elephant calf. In fact, it has already played a vital role in rescuing orphaned elephants and a baby rhino. It has been pivotal in numerous veterinary treatments, transporting our teams directly to the patient's side, and also in deploying Anti-Poaching Teams and the Canine Unit.

If planes are the workhorses, helicopters are the thoroughbreds. Getting our first helicopter was a game-changer. Its versatility is unparalleled: In anti-poaching operations, it drops our sniffer dogs and handlers at the most remote sites. In human-wildlife conflict operations, it shepherds wildlife back into parks and reserves. During fire-fighting efforts — of which there are dozens in any given year — it drops water on fires with a Bambi Bucket. For our veterinarians, it provides a perfect platform to dart injured wildlife from the air. It conducts medical evacuations of injured personnel, taking them directly from the field to the hospital. It has even played a starring role in rescuing and transporting orphaned wildlife. (The rescue of Apollo stands out as one of its most memorable missions: Not only was it an extremely challenging operation, but transporting a small but very spirited rhino by air made for quite a harrowing ride! Fortunately, our pilots and Keepers have nerves of steel.)

Helicopters and airplanes are only as good as the pilots at their helm. Our pilots are world-class, with exceptional bush prowess. They can navigate Tsavo's tempestuous winds, shepherd a herd of marauding elephants back to safety, pick out a poacher's hideout amidst the undergrowth, or even track an orphaned elephant's tiny footprints along a sandy riverbank. To my immense pride, David's nephew, Neville Sheldrick, and my sons, Taru and Roan, are accomplished pilots now, flying both fixed-wing aircraft and helicopters in the same wilderness their grandfather patrolled more than half a century ago.

Equally important is the team who keeps our aircraft in flight. Our incredibly talented engineers know every inch of these machines, inside and out. In our line of work, every day comes with unforeseen assignments and emergencies. It is our engineers based in Kaluku who ensure that our aircraft are always ready for their next mission. Our operations room, meanwhile, is the vital link between ground and air. They liaise between all the key players, be it organising a veterinary treatment or connecting the dots for an anti-poaching operation.

There's a reason I always wanted to hang out on the airstrip as a child: It really is where all the action happens. The Kaluku airstrip is always alive with activity, even when planes aren't coming and going. It has become a favourite haunt of our orphans: Apollo uses it as his own personal racetrack, while our motley crew of hooved orphans prefer to stroll up and down its length. Even local wildlife have adopted the Kaluku airstrip as a trusted thoroughfare. Just the other week, an elephant mum and her newborn baby walked by the hanger, followed by a much larger herd the following day. On both occasions, our engineers were mere steps away, working on the aircraft that take flight every day to secure the Tsavo Conservation Area.

The rescue of Kerrio shows what a world of difference an aircraft can make. It was an incredibly challenging operation to begin with, set against the backdrop of the warring Pokot and Marakwet tribes. Gunfire had broken out in the night, and by morning, a tiny elephant calf was left behind in the panic. KWS had sheltered her in the relative safety of a nearby school, but we knew this was a rescue without a moment to spare.

Navigating thunderous storms, the helicopter made the turbulent journey north. No sooner had it touched down onsite than the elephant was loaded inside, hooked up to an IV drip, and on her way back to the sanctuary of our Nairobi Nursery. Without these aerial capabilities, Kerrio's rescue would have been simply impossible: Chesogon is a very remote corner of Kenya, and such a vulnerable orphan would have never survived such a demanding journey by road. She is alive today because of that helicopter we were able to charter, given that this rescue happened at the opposite end of the country to our Tsavo operations.

The value our Aerial Unit brings to the table is priceless. It is quantified, to me, by every life saved: orphans we were miraculously able to locate and rescue from this vast wilderness, veterinary cases we could rapidly respond to which would otherwise prove impossible to treat, roaming elephants we were able to spare from human-wildlife conflict, untold numbers of wildlife threatened by bushfires we managed to extinguish, even gravely injured rangers who we were able to transport to hospital. These individual stories tell a much larger tale, one of how success in the sky translates to extraordinary impact on the ground.

5Y-STP

SECOND CHANCES AND A WILD FUTURE

— August 2019 —

Sometimes, things come together in a truly unexpected way, as if by divine intervention. When Umani Springs and the Kibwezi Forest fell into the safe hands of the SWT, it very much felt like that. We were faced with a spectacular responsibility and opportunity: To protect and transform this natural paradise and, by extension, create a fitting sanctuary for the orphaned elephants we rescue who are permanently damaged by the cruel hand of fate. This beautiful area and its unique orphan herd are a great example of how, when given a second chance, the natural world can recover, heal, and flourish against great odds.

All of Kenya's wild spaces hold their own magic, but the Kibwezi Forest is a true gem. Within its heart, this unique groundwater forest safeguards a network of springs that percolate out of lava banks, snaking between the reaching roots of giant fig trees, and tumbling into crystalline ponds. It is truly the life force behind all residents in the area, from the forest's endemic species to the orphaned elephants who are healing there to the communities that live along its borders.

But it was not always this way. The opportunity to fund, manage, and protect the Kibwezi Forest came to us in 2008, when we undertook a long-term lease from the Kenya Forest Service as part of our Saving Habitats Program. After visiting the area, Daphne's words were, "I honestly cannot see the potential." — that is how degraded and denuded the forest was back in that time. It was easy to see her point: Kibwezi had been completely ravaged by bushmeat poaching, illegal logging, charcoal harvesting, and livestock incursions.

However, we never step down from a challenge. On signing the agreement, our first step was to secure the boundary with a substantial electric fence, which connected the Kibwezi Forest on three sides into the Chyulu Hills National Park, and then continue that fenceline for 74 more kilometres along the border of the National Park's boundary. We employed 45 members of the community to patrol daily, working with our dedicated staff to ensure that this ambitious project was maintained. We continue to support the Kenya Wildlife Service's management of the Chyulu Hills National Park with two anti-poaching teams that operate in the area, along with aerial surveillance, fire control, donation of vehicles and the funding and management of the fenceline.

The effects of these efforts have been nothing short of transformative: With the forest's boundary secure, the community is safe from human-wildlife conflict and the ecosystem within is shielded from the ravages of man. It is a graphic example of nature's extraordinary powers of recovery when it is protected. In the past decade, wildlife populations have blossomed, the vegetation has recovered, and rainfall has increased year over year. Daphne witnessed this extraordinary recovery, and Umani Springs soon became one of her favourite places to visit.

In 2014, we once again tapped into the magic of the Kibwezi Forest — this time to provide hope to some very special miracles, elephant orphans who came to us with the odds stacked against them. Many of these orphans, like Murera and Sonje, had suffered from horrendous poaching injuries that left them permanently compromised. We needed a special place for them to heal, flourish, and eventually, transition to a wild life. The Kibwezi Forest, with its gentle environment and high security, seemed a most fitting destination for all of that to come to fruition.

It is a challenge to begin a Reintegration Unit from scratch, without the continuity of older and wiser wild-living orphans to mentor new arrivals. When Murera and Sonje arrived as the first residents of Umani Springs, they were extremely unsettled. Thankfully, it was only for two days before the next group of orphans arrived. Quanza, Lima Lima, and Zongoloni were bonded friends, and while they all held psychological scars from the events that left them orphaned, theirs were not physical.

From the moment she disembarked from the transporter truck, it became evident that Lima Lima was the glue that would hold the Umani herd together. This remarkable elephant immediately embraced her new home with a passion that was infectious. While Murera and Sonje were the older two, Lima Lima provided the enthusiasm and leadership that the rest of the group initially needed. Something about the forest had a transformative effect on her; she had been a rather colourless character at the Nursery, but suddenly her spirit soared and she exhibited a joie de vivre that the other orphans couldn't help but also embody.

Over the years at Umani, Lima Lima continues to amaze us. Not only is she the nexus for this orphan group, but she has also taken it upon herself to be the protector of the Keepers. This new environment was as foreign to them as it was to their charges, but Lima Lima assumed full responsibility of ensuring their safety — a duty she cheerfully takes on each and every day.

Sometimes, when they find they are lost in the forest's dense undergrowth, she steps up and guides the whole group home. She has an innate ability to spot danger and is always the first to alert the Keepers of the presence of buffalos, wild elephants, or anything she perceives as potentially hazardous for the men. Murera and Sonje remain the matriarchs of Umani, but they were robbed of the physical capacity to lead from the front, so Lima Lima has taken on the role of their deputy. This energetic elephant, who is brimming with love for her elephant and human family, defers to her matriarchs and ensures Umani's continued success.

It is also special to note the equalising power of Umani Springs: While many of its orphans are physically compromised, they are always relocated with their closest confidants from the Nursery, as we would never dream of having them embark on a wild life without their best friends by their sides. As such, many of the Umani orphans are not injured at all — but in reality, none of the orphans there feel like special needs elephants any more, despite the fact that many still carry the physical scars of their past. They are all happily thriving, deeply bonded to each other and their Keepers, while also forging successful friendships with the wild elephant community.

I began Umani Springs with a handful of trusted, long-serving Keepers. At the time, I imagined that they would remain there just long enough to settle the establishment, before returning to circulate between our many other facilities. However, the Kibwezi Forest has a magnetic hold over all those who cross under its leafy canopy. Being cocooned in this special, natural world, surrounded by elephants who are the beating heart and soul of Umani Springs, proved too important a bond to disturb — and it seems I have happily lost these Keepers to this haven forever! I can think of no more certain measure of success.

Through perseverance, hard work, and unwavering belief, the Kibwezi Forest has been wrestled back from the brink of destruction. Today, it is a peaceful and protected Utopia, affording a viable, wild future to the special miracles who also needed a second chance.

A JOURNEY THROUGH PAST AND PRESENT

— November 2022 —

"Stepping back in time, we glimpse the world of yesterday, and we will be reminded that we share it with many other creatures who are also a part of creation with a specific purpose to their being, a vital link in the chain of life. Then thinking of the wonders all around us, we become mindful also of a great responsibility that has been vested in us, the responsibility to keep the chain of life intact, for to break a link is to jeopardise our own survival and that of many other creatures too. Suddenly things fall into place and we begin to understand a little more about living, and a little more about ourselves."

– Daphne Sheldrick, writing about Tsavo –

2022 marked the Trust's 45th anniversary, but our conservation story dates back to the first half of the twentieth century. In 1948, my father, David Sheldrick, was appointed the founding warden of Tsavo East National Park. David was ahead of his time in so many ways: He was a passionate naturalist, with an ambitious vision for habitat preservation and wildlife conservation.

This was before poaching had decimated elephant and rhino populations across Africa. During his aerial patrols, it was a common sight for David to see aggregate elephant herds numbering well into the thousands. As a child, I remember how the park was teeming with rhinos; you could barely go a kilometre without an encounter.

While we will never recover the populations of days gone by, I know David and his team would be proud of the progress made today. African elephants are endangered across the continent, but their numbers have been climbing in Kenya. The catastrophic poaching era of the late 1970s to early 1990s saw their population plummet to 6,000. Today, there are estimated to be 15,000-16,000 elephants in Tsavo. Drought years like this do take their toll, but there are signs of hope: Where rain has recently fallen, our pilots have seen large breeding herds that number into the hundreds beginning to aggregate, which is always a most welcome sight.

Even back then, David and his team recognised the fragility of our natural world. Beginning in the 1960s, they started extensive anti-poaching campaigns in the landscape. Showing remarkable prescience, David put great emphasis on aerial patrols. Today, his grandsons and other talented pilots fly over the same landscape he covered more than 60 years ago.

It is difficult to grasp the vastness of Tsavo. It is Kenya's largest National Park and a relic from an ancient world, one where wildlife still reigns. David and his team realised that connectivity was paramount to successful conservation in the landscape. They set about creating infrastructure in harmony with the wilderness, including a network of roads that became vital arteries for field teams stationed in the park. In these early days, roads had to first be cut by hand, with no elaborate equipment available to clear huge swathes of dense commiphora bush.

Planning the road network was all done on foot, which was an extremely dangerous undertaking — back then, Tsavo was home to some 8,000 black rhinos, which could come hurtling out of the bush at any moment. I recall many dramatic stories of rangers scaling trees or anthills in an effort to escape charging rhinos. One ranger was even dragged for 800 metres by a rhino, its horn hooked between his webbing belt. Fortunately, and miraculously, his story had a happy ending.

Through the sands of time, many of David's original routes in the remote northern area of Tsavo fell into disrepair. However, the tourism lull during the pandemic provided a perfect window for the Trust to concentrate its support and help rehabilitate northern Tsavo's infrastructure — and as a result, hundreds of kilometres of old roads were resurrected. These paths are not a relic of the past, but a reminder of how much in conservation is timeless. Rhinos may no longer pop out from around every corner, but much remains unchanged. Age-old routes provide vital connectivity, unlocking parts of the park for security field teams and visitors alike. During the drought, enhanced accessibility made a world of difference, as teams ramped up patrols and responded to an increase in field emergencies.

Many of these field emergencies are echoes of the past. New eras usher in new threats — first poaching, now human-wildlife conflict — but there has always been, and will always be, animals in need of help. David and his team were masters in outside-the-box thinking, be it charting complex ambushes to catch poachers or rigging up clever ways to rescue elephants bogged in drying waterholes.

We apply that same outside-the-box thinking to everything we do today. This year stretched even the most imaginative minds, as the drought brought unique challenges to the fore. Countless creatures got stuck in muddy mires, but none more so than elephants. From a set of bulls to a mum and baby, our teams moved heaven and earth to save giant lives. Just this week, they dug an emergency exit for two giraffes trapped in a trench — and rescued a surprise orphan in the process.

And that brings me to our beginnings: the orphans. It was in Tsavo that David met Daphne, sparking a great love — but even more so, a magnificent partnership, the meeting of two people who were far ahead of their time.

As David and Daphne built upon a shared vision of conservation, they also raised the first elephant orphans, creating the basis for what would become our pioneering Orphans' Project. Near their field headquarters, they constructed the first stockades, which still stand today as part of our Voi Reintegration Unit. Today, Voi continues to be home to many of our orphans, and to new generations of elephants, as ex-orphans and their wild-born babies visit periodically. Daphne and David created a life together in Voi. I was born and raised in Tsavo East, growing up alongside an eclectic assortment of orphaned wildlife. My wild upbringing continued in Nairobi National Park, where we moved in 1976.

But tragedy struck the following year, when David died of a heart attack. While his life was cut short, Daphne was determined that his legacy live on. She founded the Sheldrick Wildlife Trust in his memory. She also established the Nairobi Nursery, creating a home for Kenya's infant orphaned elephants and further honing the husbandry to successfully raise them.

To date, we have successfully raised more than 300 orphaned elephants, along with an assortment of rhinos, giraffes, and other wildlife. From the Nursery's humble beginnings, we now have five orphan locations, including three Reintegration Units where older orphans reclaim their place in the wild.

Daphne always said that her greatest wish was to see offspring born to orphans raised by our hand. That wish has been delivered more than 60 times over, and of course there are many more out there — the baby boom is just beginning. We already have 'great-grandkids' in Voi, and we just sprouted that new branch on our Ithumba family tree, meeting the first calf born to the offspring of an orphan raised there.

In difficult years like this one, the orphans help me keep things in perspective: While fate brought them into our care, they grow up blissfully sheltered. As the drought swept across Kenya, they remained stalwartly consumed by their own daily dramas: Who got the first milk bottle? What mysterious creature is hiding in the bush? Is the feed store really as impenetrable as it seems? It is our privilege to shield these little creatures through their infancy, allowing them to fully indulge in the minutiae. Reality will set in, as it does for all of us. But in the meantime, we can give these orphans the carefree, loving upbringing that every youngster deserves. All the while, we are working across Kenya to protect their wild counterparts and preserve the habitats they will one day call home.

This is the work David and Daphne began more than 45 years ago. Working alongside my family and our incredible team, I am proud to bring their vision into the future. The world has changed enormously since the Trust's inception. But in the ways that matter, it remains exactly the same.

LUGGARD THE LIONHEART

— June 2020 —

It's a call I will always remember. On 31st March 2016, one of our pilots set out for a routine aerial patrol over Tsavo East. It transpired to be anything but: Mid-flight, he spotted a four-month-old calf with a broken leg, who was struggling to keep up with his herd. His injuries were mortal, and it was clear that he didn't have much longer to live without veterinary intervention.

When the calf arrived at the Nursery, my heart sank. His injuries, which were already a few weeks old, had been caused by a hail of bullets. An X-ray revealed that his right femur was shattered, while another bullet had pierced his left foot. Because of the time elapsed and proximity of the femur injury to the knee joint, combined with the muscle override, operating on or pinning his bone was impossible. It was clear that we would have a gruelling challenge on our hands to save him.

In these cases, we can try our hardest to save the calf, but they also must have the steely determination to survive. Despite all the odds stacked against him, he had this in spades. From the moment we met him, we were struck by his fiercely bright alert eyes and his stoic bravery. In fact, it was largely through sheer willpower that he had even come this far. This galvanised us all to move mountains to save him, despite the fact that his initial prognosis looked very bleak indeed. We called him Luggard, after the area where he was rescued, but his character quickly earned him the nickname "Luggard the Lionheart."

It's horrible to witness pain and suffering, least of all in such a young, innocent creature. In Luggard's case, time and strength of mind were the only antidotes. What we could provide was a wonderfully nurturing environment, along with lengthy treatments to stave off infection and motivate his own body to go into healing mode.

There were some small mercies: A hind leg injury in elephants is always preferable to a front leg injury, as walking on three legs is easier when you have the use of both front, weight-bearing legs. In this regard, Luggard was fortunate. His was not a clean break, so his body would periodically expel bone chips in little pustules. Because Luggard's body was battling infection for years, he remained rather stunted, and it wasn't long before his age-mates began to dwarf him.

It is easy to become preoccupied by the injustices of Luggard's circumstances, but his story is ultimately one of resilience and hope. Given his impediments, he spent much of his four years at the Nursery in the company of younger orphans and new rescues. However, his beautiful soul endeared him to all who knew him, and each member of the Nursery herd had a special place in their heart for Luggard. We saw evidence of this every day: The usually boisterous bulls would temper their wrestling games so Luggard could join in; members of the herd would hang back to walk at his slower pace; Maxwell the rhino would joyfully bound up to meet him at his gate in the morning.

As the years wore on, Luggard's friendships continued to evolve. Many were forged through shared challenges. He grew close with Enkesha, who knew her fair share of pain from the snare that nearly severed her trunk; Ziwadi, who struggled with seizures for months after her rescue, became another dear friend.

Because of his unusual situation, Luggard's circle of friends has transcended elephants and he became the babysitter to orphans of all shapes and sizes. During Kiko the giraffe's early days at the Nursery, it was Luggard who browsed in his company. Being his nighttime

neighbour was a coveted role: For years, he slept with Musiara on one side and Kiko on the other. Kiko's customised, giraffe-sized stable was fitted with a special window into Luggard's room, so the pair could fraternise. The giraffe became so attached to his neighbour that any later attempts to move him into a larger stockade were futile, as Kiko would fret without Luggard's company! When Musiara finally outgrew his stable and moved into a stockade, we removed the stable partitions so our little Lionheart could have a scrumptiously large area to call his own.

Luggard also forged a permanent place in our Keepers' hearts.They dedicated so much time to healing him, both physically and emotionally, and played an integral role in his survival. So, it was a bittersweet moment indeed when we realised that Luggard was ready to take his next step in his reintegration journey and say goodbye to the Nursery. The signs were obvious, as they are with all our orphans who are ready to graduate: By then, he was by far the oldest boy at the Nursery and seemed to have a bit of ennui because of it. He was clearly at a stage where he would benefit from the stimulation and guidance of older elephants.

While Tsavo was his birthplace, Luggard was no longer physically equipped to thrive there. Elephants follow the rains, and during Tsavo's brutal dry seasons, they are often required to travel vast distances for both water and food. Luggard needed a gentler environment, a lush place he could call home throughout the year. Luckily, we have just the spot: Our Umani Springs Reintegration Unit, situated within the Kibwezi Forest, was purpose-built for special-needs elephants and their friends. Kibwezi is a groundwater forest we have a concession to manage and protect, with sparkling springs and leafy vegetation throughout the year. It is part of our Saving Habitat Program, managed and stringently protected in a public private partnership with the Kenya Forest Service.

On the morning of 31st of May 2020, we bundled up our precious cargo and bid Nairobi farewell. Luggard graduated in the company of Enkesha, his dear friend and fellow survivor. It was a date we approached with no small measure of apprehension, but we needn't have worried. Both elephants handled the proceedings like pros, breezing into the elephant moving lorry and snacking their way to the Kibwezi Forest. Upon arrival, they were met with nothing short of a rapturous welcome.

Watching this all unfold was a special moment indeed. Seeing our young Lionheart confidently stride off the truck and into the Umani Springs fold was in such stark contrast to the helpless, nearly lifeless form who was carried into the Nursery four years ago. The members of Luggard's new herd intuitively knew that he needed additional attention and focus. He quickly became the most pampered member of the Umani family.

Any violence against elephants is unfathomable, but it boggles the mind as to how such a young calf fell under a hail of bullets. Perhaps Luggard got caught in the crosshairs of human-wildlife conflict, or was the unintended recipient of a poaching attempt. While we may never know or understand the circumstances that befell him, we can comfort ourselves in the fact that we gave him a good life for the five years he was with us.

In the early hours of 11th May 2021, Luggard left us. His death was sudden but not wholly unsurprising. In the months leading up to his passing, his condition started to deteriorate. We consulted a slate of vets, but each test brought more questions than answers. In the end, we believe that his body had simply taken him as far as it could go.

We wish more than anything that Luggard's story had ended differently, but we know that his time with us was unfalteringly happy to the very end: His blissful little rumbles, brought upon by something as simple as a trunk hug or an ear rub, communicated that loud and clear. Now, his heavenly spirit will forever preside over the herd who so cherished him.

DROUGHT COMES TO TSAVO

— August 2022 —

Left to its own devices, nature is a severe but just master. Some years, abundance prevails; others, it withholds its bounty, and the environment goes without. This is the natural order of things, a finely tuned system that has sustained our planet for millions of years.

Nowhere is the natural order more evident than in Africa, where all life hinges on the seasonal rains. It just takes a few good storms to reinvigorate the landscape. However, rain is a fickle beast. Even building clouds on the horizon aren't a given; shifting ocean currents and monsoon winds can dissolve that hope in an instant.

In 1970-71, Tsavo fell into the grips of a devastating drought. 6,000 elephants lost their lives during that period — but far from spelling long-term disaster, the drought balanced wildlife populations. My father, David Sheldrick, was the warden of Tsavo at the time. I was just a child, but I still remember him dealing with the devastation, while explaining that this was nature at its most brutal.

Now, we must contend with a rogue factor: Climate change has shifted the natural order of things, disrupting age-old weather patterns and throwing a finely tuned system into disarray. Rains are failing with increasing regularity, driving soaring temperatures and more frequent droughts. Wildlife have evolved to survive in the landscape in which they live. The occasional anomaly can actually benefit a species — the weak succumb to a drought; the strong prevail — but when the natural order changes, they are left grappling with a world they are not adapted to. This is compounded by the human factor: shrinking rangelands, competition over limited resources, and the resultant human-wildlife conflict.

Tsavo is one of Africa's greatest remaining wildernesses and the largest National Park in Kenya. Amidst shrinking landscapes, it remains a rich, viable habitat for all manner of creatures. Two years ago, Tsavo was blessed with a period of abundance. The landscape was green as far as the eye could see. The old prospered and the young proliferated. Elephants, those giant barometers of the ecosystem, stood tall and healthy. Each herd had a bevy of plump, round-cheeked babies frolicking in their midst.

But how quickly good fortune can flip. Poor rains last year brought Tsavo to the brink of a drought; failed rains earlier this year sealed its fate. Resident wildlife are hanging on as best they can. This isn't the first time they have faced difficult times, nor will it be the last. Like most of Africa's great wildernesses, Tsavo has always been a demanding landscape.

Plains that were once verdant and buzzing have fallen still. The blanket of green has transformed into parched earth, the expanse of red only broken by well-trod paths to remaining watering points. Yet, life prevails. Giraffes reach high into the acacia trees, plucking precious leaves with their long tongues. Lions laze in the shade, resting before the next hunt. Game congregates around water sources, creating a melting pot of African life as creatures great and small patiently wait their turn for a drink.

And of course, the elephants forge ahead. Tsavo's great matriarchs and bulls are no strangers to adversity. Elephants have faced a disproportionate share of hardship in the past century, both manmade — hunting, ivory poaching, habitat loss — and naturally induced. Some were even alive to witness the great drought of 1970. Etched into the deepest recesses of their brains is the wisdom needed to navigate these periods. They have a unique ability to sniff out water sources, even subterranean streams that are invisible to the naked eye. Following ancient migratory paths, they can root out places where vegetation still thrives. A successful elephant will balance generations' worth of knowledge with in-the-moment decisiveness, knowing when to follow their ancestors and when to forge their own path.

Elephants are an incredibly complex, intelligent species — and they need all their wits about them to weather a drought. It is a great irony that the world's mightiest animal is also the most vulnerable to periods of want. But again, this is the natural order at work. In an ideal

world, elephants would have few threats to their survival. To compensate, nature has made them fragile. They have poor digestion and require prodigious quantities of vegetation to sustain themselves. In a drought, it is a lack of food, more so than a lack of water, that has fatal consequences.

As human actions have disrupted the natural order, it is up to us to balance the scales. Long before this drought set in, we have been working to help landscapes better support wildlife amidst our changing climate. While water initiatives may not capture the same level of attention as our other conservation projects, they are equally vital to a functioning ecosystem. Our Water for Wildlife project brings tailored water solutions to arid areas, providing a lifeline to animals during the dry season and unlocking areas that were previously uninhabitable for much of the year.

Typically, these solutions take the form of boreholes. Where aquifers are plentiful, but surface drinking water is scarce, boreholes tap into water tables deep beneath the ground. We strategically install them far from communities, drawing wildlife deeper into the protection of the park. Boreholes also supply the hard-working teams who are positioned in these conservation areas.

Water projects can transform a landscape, as one of our more recent installations demonstrates. Located in the northern sector of Tsavo East, Thabagunji was a vast, pristine wilderness with one notable problem: Its natural water pans dry up, forcing most creatures to leave during the dry season. Two years ago, we were able to change that. We installed a borehole in the heart of the landscape, which feeds into three different water pans and a large trough. Once news spread that fresh water was now available and food plentiful, wildlife quickly migrated to the area. Even now, at the height of the drought, herds are benefitting from this more plentiful landscape.

This is a time when wildlife needs us most. As we implement sustainable, long-term support, we must also be ready to help at a moment's notice. Field emergencies are unfolding on a daily basis. The influx of orphans that began last year has not abated; indeed, it will likely only increase as the drought continues to take hold. More often than not, human-wildlife conflict — compounded by drought — is the reason elephants are orphaned during this time. Competition over resources is fraught, and elephants are sometimes forced to leave protected areas in search of food, where danger ensues. But sometimes, matriarchs must make heartbreaking decisions. Elephants know they must prioritise the herd's survival above any individual. When the weak slip behind, the strong press on. Calves are vulnerable, and they are often the first to fall.

This drought has already claimed too many lives. Unlike the drought of 1970, Kenya's elephant population is not at max capacity. Instead, there has been a concerted effort to nurture its numbers, which plummeted in the 1980s due to ivory poaching. The turn of the 21st century brought another population dip, between a resurgence in ivory poaching and the expanding human footprint. These orphans are the lucky ones, spared in the nick of time. While they very nearly lost their futures, they will now grow up supported by a loving human-elephant family, until they are ready to reclaim their place among Tsavo's wild herds.

It is not only Kenya's smallest elephants who need our help. As I mentioned earlier, elephants are among the drought's most vulnerable victims. Their sheer size is the culprit. Along with the vast quantities of food they need to sustain themselves, their body weight easily gets them stuck. As they venture into drying water pans for a drink or a wallow, one misstep turns into a lethal trap. In the past month alone, we have rescued four adult elephants from such situations. This is a Herculean task. There is no shortcut to free an elephant; usually, our teams must crawl in the mud, manually digging around the poor creature to secure ropes that can haul them out.

These field emergencies are quite incredible. Imagine how stressful it must be for a wild elephant to be completely trapped, as men and vehicles converge around them. And yet, they remain cooperative throughout, clearly understanding that we are there to help. If one ever needed a reminder of the cognisance of elephants, this is a stunning example.

Even in times of hardship, hope prevails. One of our most recent field operations brought this into stark relief. It was a difficult undertaking to free this particular bull, as he had slipped deep into the mud of a drying dam and was stuck fast. Day turned into night, and it wasn't until 10 PM that the team finally pulled him onto solid ground. He was weakened by his ordeal and struggled to stand. Almost as if on cue, a wild herd arrived at the dam. Everyone retreated to let the elephants drink in peace — but instead, they gathered around the recumbent bull and helped him to his feet. Ensconced by his friends, he disappeared into the darkness, free at last.

Life in Tsavo isn't easy right now, to be sure. But elephants are remarkable creatures. They have navigated great challenges before, and they will do so again. The next few months will be difficult, but we cling to hope that rains are waiting on the other side. Until the heavens open, we will be there, as we always have been — doing our very best to provide support through these trying times.

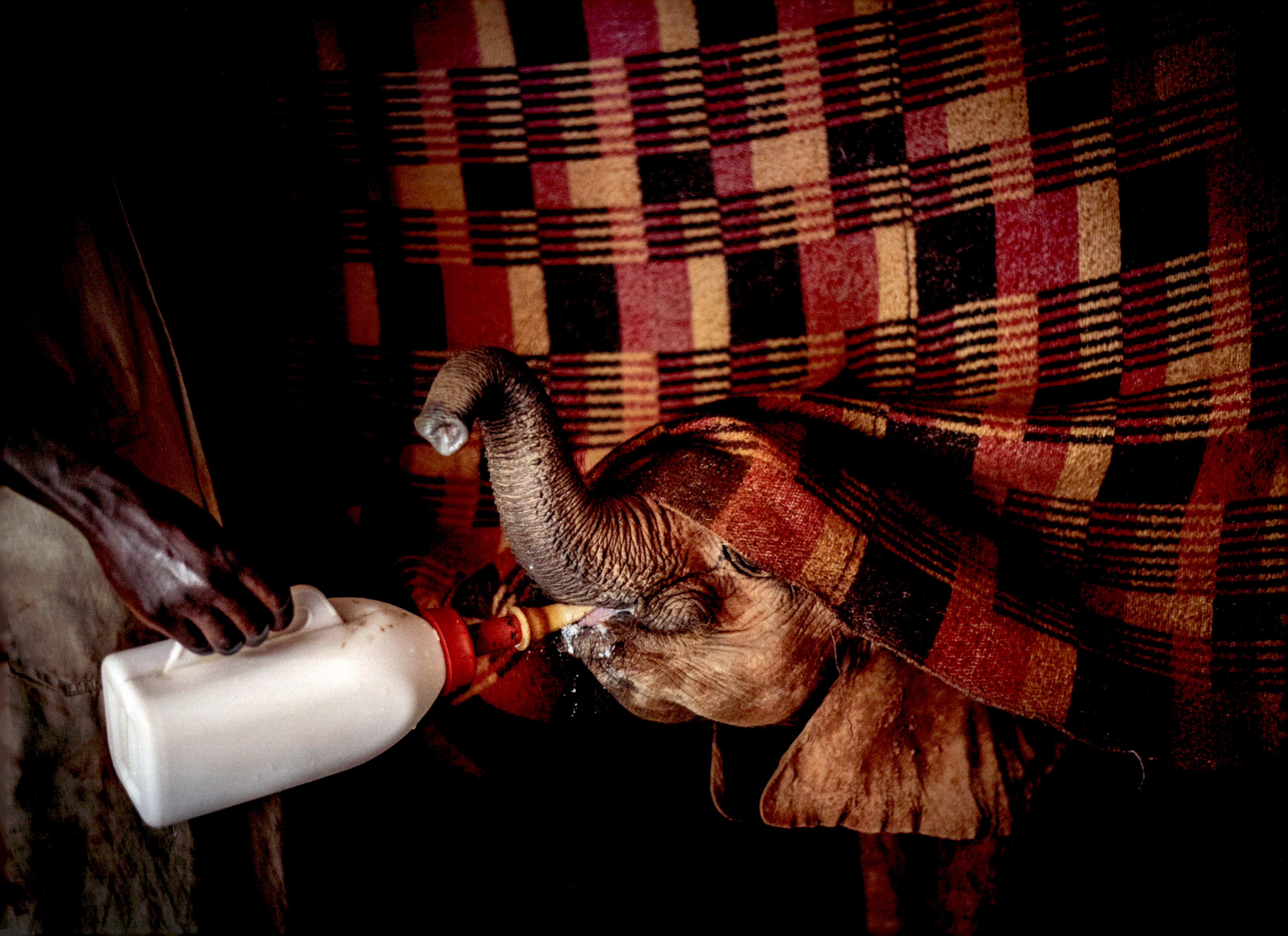

HOW OUR NEONATE NURSERY CAME TO BE

— May 2021 —

Our Kaluku Neonate Nursery feels like my mother's parting gift: Its foundation was totally unexpected yet perfectly serendipitous, and with one ending came new beginnings. Just as Daphne's brave battle with cancer was coming to an end in 2018, two new orphans entered the fold. Both were females, startlingly young elephants who had overcome incredible odds to even survive the circumstances that left them orphaned. It was not lost on any of us that, had it not been for Daphne's pioneering work, these girls would have never had a chance.

However, the odds were still stacked against them. Orphans this young always make one's heart sink. Raising any infant elephant is a formidable task, but for a true neonate to survive is a feat indeed. As my mother once said, "Baby elephants are extremely fragile. They can be fine one day and dead the next. That is where experience comes in—just being able to detect any such signs early enough to do something about it."

These decades of experience are what led us to Kaluku. At the time, much of Kenya was experiencing daily storms. Rivers were bursting their banks and cars were getting washed off the roads in Nairobi National Park. Our Nairobi Nursery was right in the thick of it, receiving as much as five inches of rain in a single deluge, day after day. As a result, the Nursery was inescapably sodden, cold, and overcast, with rain soaking every corner leaving the compound saturated — hardly an oasis in which to bring newly rescued neonate elephants.

Lemeki was the first to arrive — and what an entrance she made. On 20th March 2018, rangers spotted a tiny elephant floundering in the Mara River. While she seemed remarkably unperturbed by her watery odyssey (we would later come to realise that nonchalance is a Lemeki signature!), we recognised that appearances could be deceiving: This calf was no more than a week old and, given her age and prolonged time in the river, dangerously susceptible to pneumonia. Bringing her to Nairobi simply wasn't an option.

And so, we changed course and flew Lemeki directly to our Kaluku Field HQ in Tsavo, which was warm and — crucially — dry. We never expected to raise elephants at Kaluku. It is the head of all our field work, the nexus of our anti-poaching, mobile veterinary, aerial surveillance, habitat preservation, and community outreach operations. Over the years, we had raised an assortment of orphaned wildlife there, but never elephants. There had simply never been a need to divert from Nairobi. However, the floods of 2018 changed all that.

When we woke up that morning, we never could have imagined that a neonate elephant would be arriving at Kaluku's doorstep. As a result, little Lemeki got a hastily cobbled together welcoming committee — not that she seemed to notice. She emerged from the rescue helicopter larger than life, owning her new environment from the outset and thriving in the warm climate of Tsavo. She immediately reigned over Kaluku as if it was her own little kingdom, brightening everyone's days with her dramas and demands.

While we set about building elephant stables at Kaluku, Lemeki took up residence in a ground-floor office that had been converted into a makeshift bedroom. No sooner had we gotten to work on her accommodations, however, then another neonate came into our care. On the afternoon of 2nd April 2018, Kindani was spotted alone in Meru National Park. Just days old — too young to know fear, but acutely aware she needed a family — she eagerly followed the KWS rangers who found her. She too had a slim chance of survival at Nairobi, but given the late hour, we couldn't transport her all the way down to Tsavo that night. So, while our Kaluku team prepared for yet another arrival, Kindani enjoyed a brief stopover in Nairobi, where she was swaddled in extra thick blankets to ward off the chill.

Given Kindani and Lemeki's respective precarious states, we knew how risky it would be to put them in close quarters. Baby elephants can carry all manner of illnesses, so immediate close contact could inadvertently put one at risk from the other. While Lemeki took up residence closer to the field operations, we put Kindani in a small stable block close to my family's house.

Things got more complicated when the Athi River, which runs past Kaluku, burst its banks one night, engulfing Kindani's stable in water. Thinking fast as waters began to rise, her Keepers took her up to our home, which sits on much higher ground overlooking the river. For a full nine hours, the house remained a marooned island and fully inaccessible. Kindani and her Keepers spent a rather sleepless night in Daphne's bedroom. Those floods experienced that night were the most dramatic recorded on this river in 100 years. Numerous properties along the river were flooded and lost to the raging waters that night, our Galdessa Lodge being one of them.

I still marvel at how everything came together at this moment. I really believe my mother was watching over us. You see, Daphne passed away on the 12th April. She bore witness to the very beginnings of our Kaluku Neonate Nursery and was absolutely delighted by this solution to raise our most vulnerable orphans. The fact that, just days after her death, a baby elephant ended up slumbering in her bedroom — well, it felt like a sign from above.

While Daphne would have happily donated her bedroom to Kindani, it was hardly a long-term solution. As soon as the weather allowed, we rebuilt and expanded her stable block. It was a good thing, too, for in the following months, several more neonate orphans would come into our care. Kindani's herd expanded to include Kinyei, who was found skirting around a pride of lions, and Bondeni, who wandered into a village bordering the Chyulu Hills. Lemeki, meanwhile, reigned over the whole other side of Kaluku. Her little herd grew, too.

Raising infant orphans requires a completely customised approach: There is no "one-size-fits-all" method when it comes to baby elephants. This is especially true when it comes to neonates. Because new rescues continued to filter in, each more vulnerable than the next, we kept Lemeki and Kindani's groups separate, so as to not put newcomers at risk.

This also allowed us to provide extremely tailored care to each group. For instance, after two years at Kaluku, we recognised that Kindani, Kinyei, and Bondeni would benefit from the influence of older orphans. With this in mind, we moved them to our Nairobi Nursery in September 2020. I am happy to report they are thriving there — Kindani and Kinyei, who are both quite introverted, are making new friends at their own pace, while our little extrovert Bondeni has taken the entire Nursery by storm.

Lemeki, on the other hand, prefers to be the queen of her own kingdom. She is a bit more advanced than the other members of her herd, three young bulls who are unabashedly devoted to her. We knew that if we were to move her to Nairobi, it would send her little charges into disarray. Aside from that, Lemeki didn't seem to be wanting for socialisation in the same way that Kindani and Kinyei were. In fact, she is the definition of a mini matriarch. She lords over man and beast at Kaluku — even the resident guinea fowl trail loyally after her! For that reason, Lemeki will continue her reign at Kaluku until her friends are ready to join her at one of our Reintegration Units in Tsavo, where they will all take the next step in their journey back to the wild.

While it was born from urgent circumstances, this corner of the Tsavo Conservation Area is a perfect place to raise neonate elephants. These babies spend their days in absolute bliss, sliding down sandy lugga banks, and splashing in the still waters of a now more subdued Athi River. Their bellies are plump from the bounty of green vegetation at their disposal, while their minds are bright from the constant stimulation that comes from exploring nature's playground.

Our Kaluku Neonate Nursery came to be at a very difficult time for me, and for the Trust as a whole. Daphne was a rock to all of us. Her passing left us adrift and absolutely heartbroken. Kaluku was the balm that put it back together. Creating a solution amidst the most turbulent and challenging circumstances, saving these tiny elephant lives and giving them the future they deserved, was the most fitting way to honour my mother's legacy.

THE TRAGEDY AND TRIUMPH OF KENYA'S ELEPHANTS

— August 2020 —

To begin, we must go back in time. At the turn of the 20th century, Africa was home to about 12 million elephants. Today, some 400,000 roam the continent. In other words, over the course of a century, 97 percent of these revered creatures disappeared from the earth.

Human greed is at the root of this decline. The rise of trophy hunting put the species under strain, but the international appetite for ivory trinkets proved cataclysmic. It was a slow burn until the late 1970s, when poaching reached frenzied levels. In 1969, uncarved ivory was worth $2.50 per pound. By 1978, demand had driven the price up to $34 per pound. In a single decade, Africa lost half its elephants to the ivory trade.

This was a sobering wake up call. In July 1989, when Kenya's elephant population had dwindled to just 16,000, then-President Daniel arap Moi burned 12 tonnes of ivory to bring global attention to the poaching crisis. More than just an emblematic inferno, this was also a compelling call to action: Three months later, the international commercial ivory trade was effectively banned under the Convention on International Trade in Endangered Species (CITES).

Over the next several years, elephant populations began to recover. However, as we embarked on the new millennium, poaching remained a dormant threat. Driven by a renewed desire for ivory objects in the East, a second wave of poaching began in force. Between 2010 and 2012, one elephant was killed every 15 minutes for its ivory.

This was a harrowing time for the species, as indicated by the tragic influx of orphans we rescued during the three-year period. Some were found standing vigil beside their dying mothers (Araba, Barsilinga, Quanza, and Zongoloni stand out as four heartbreaking examples). More often than not, however, the calves were discovered completely alone, witness to untold tragedies.

As the global community rallied around elephants, we took swift action here in Kenya. Working in partnership with the KWS, we ramped up our work in the field. We expanded our anti-poaching operations, bringing on a canine unit and growing our fleet of aircraft to bolster patrols on the ground and in the air. We doubled our Mobile Veterinary Units, so we could quickly respond to wildlife emergencies. Crucially, we also secured vast tracts of wilderness, creating safe havens for elephants and other creatures.

And now, we reach the uplifting portion of our story: These measures worked. Thanks to a concerted effort by many, Kenya's elephant population has more than doubled in the past 30 years, to 34,000. As history has shown us, we cannot afford to be complacent about poaching, and there are other looming threats on the rise, such as habitat loss and human-wildlife conflict. However, because of dedicated conservation efforts, tuskers can continue their lineage, mothers can carry to term, calves can grow up in the wild, and the entire species has hope for a future.

Just last week, we were privileged to meet one of Kenya's newest elephants, a wild baby born to Lenana, an orphan whom we rescued in 2006. Lenana's personal story is one of tragedy and triumph: She was little more than a year old when she was found desperately trying to rouse her dead mother, who had succumbed to a mysterious illness.

That experience haunted Lenana, and she arrived at the Nursery terrified and grief-stricken. Time eventually healed her psychological wounds, and she poured her heart into caring for others, first at the Nursery, then at our Ithumba Reintegration Unit, and most recently as a wild elephant. When fellow ex-orphans Galana, Lualeni, and Kinna became mothers, Lenana was their chosen nanny. And so, we were absolutely delighted when it became clear that she too was destined for motherhood. Lenana could not wait to celebrate her joy with the people who raised her; her baby was still wobbly on his legs when she shepherded him to our Ithumba stockades on the evening of 22nd August 2020!

We are calling Lenana's calf Lapa, which means "moon" in Samburu. This seems a most fitting name for these times. During the darkest nights, the moon serves as a light, a beacon of hope. Humans may present the gravest threat to the survival of elephants, but we can also be part of the solution. For every life we save has a ripple effect, paving the way for future generations, and ensuring that we never know a world without elephants.

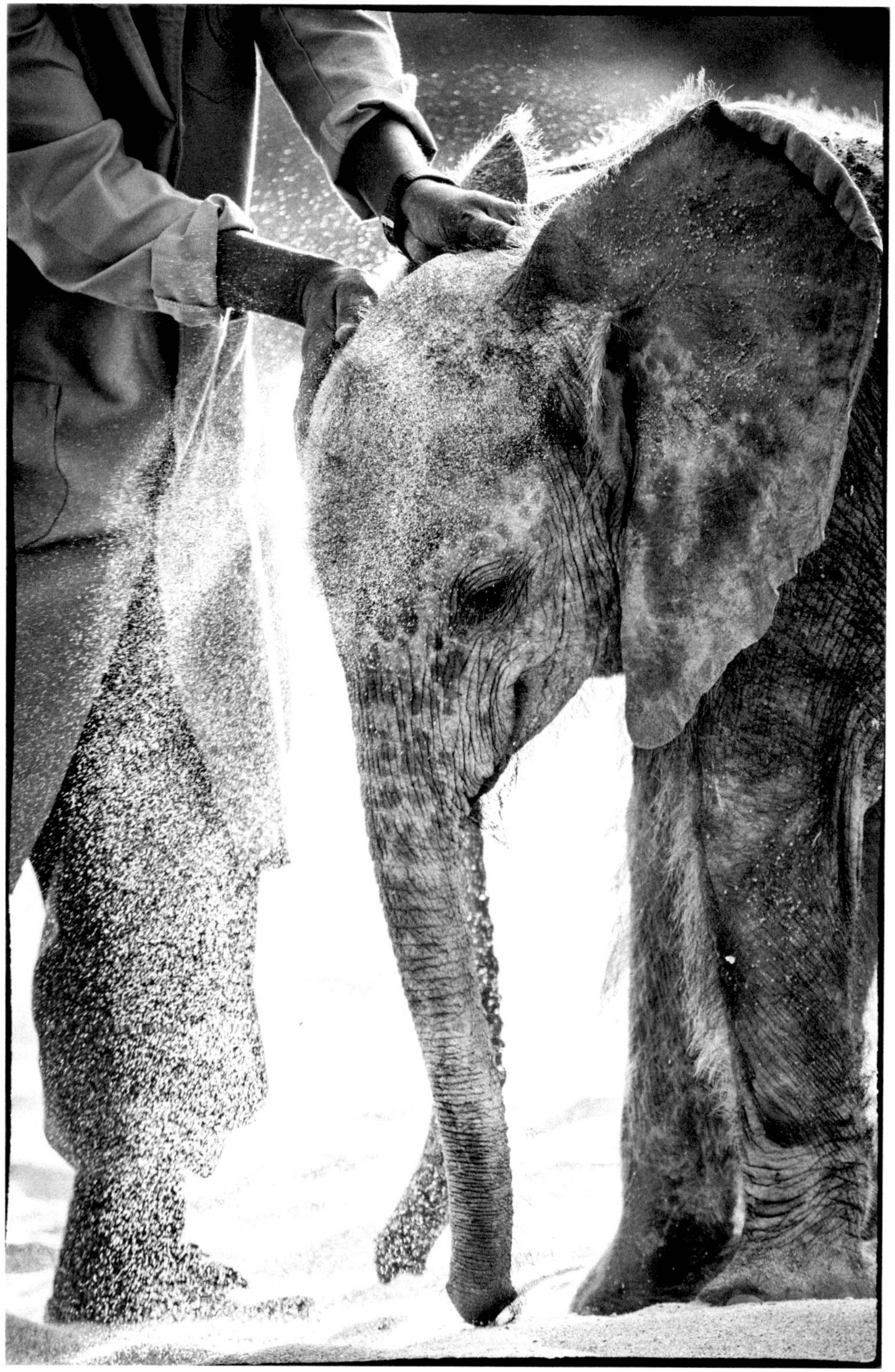

OUR LITTLE DINOSAURS

— April 2024 —

To know a baby rhino is to fall in love with them. My mother, Daphne Sheldrick, used to refer to black rhinos as 'the last living dinosaurs' — and the epithet rings true, even when it comes to the youngest generation. These little creatures are relics of an ancient, bygone era. Rhino calves are in a league of their own. Their blunt noses and button eyes give no hint to the formidable creatures they will become in a few years' time. Many of my most cherished childhood memories feature orphaned rhinos who grew up alongside me in Tsavo: Rufus greedily slurping his milk bottles, Stroppie soliciting an endless rotation of ear scratches, Hoshim flopping over for his beloved tummy rubs. To date, Sheldrick Wildlife Trust has successfully raised 19 orphaned black rhinos.

In the past two years, two new additions entered the mix: Raha stands out as our little warrior. On the afternoon of 23rd September 2022, a days-old rhino calf was discovered on her own in Ol Pejeta Conservancy. As is so often the case, much of her beginnings remain a mystery: Perhaps her mother rejected her, or else she got into an altercation with another rhino and the calf was cast aside in the process.

And then, something even more terrible happened to her. As adults, rhinos are one of the most formidable creatures in the world. However, calves are incredibly vulnerable. In the short time Raha was on her own, predators — we believe jackals — descended, leaving her mortally wounded.

It was a miracle that she survived the attack. Ol Pejeta scouts discovered her and alerted our SWT/KWS Mount Kenya Vet Unit. With the approval of Ol Pejeta and the Kenya Wildlife Service, we brought Raha to our Nairobi Nursery — ready to fight for her life, but very aware that we had an uphill battle on our hands. The predators had mauled Raha's rear end, biting her tail clean off and chewing down to the bone. At first, she wasn't even able to defecate. Thank goodness for our veterinary specialists, who painstakingly rebuilt her nether regions — and then did it all over again when the stitches collapsed. I am also eternally grateful for Raha's Keepers, who vigilantly monitored every ebb and flow in her condition, day and night. Without their dedication, she would never have survived such a precarious period.

Given the minefield that came with digestion, Raha was reluctant to eat solid food for nearly a year. But one day, something clicked, and she started tentatively chomping on the leaves hand-picked by her Keepers. The floodgates opened, and now our girl has a voracious appetite for all things green. We hang bundles of greens in her stable each night (much like an upside-down bouquet) and Raha plants herself next to them, waddling round and round as she hoovers up each successive layer.

We often joke that Raha is part tortoise. She is placid, plodding, and deliberate, doing everything at her preferred pace — and not a beat faster! Black rhinos are solitary by nature, and Raha is no exception. She shows no more than a passing interest in Maxwell (the Nursery's resident blind black rhino) and barely tolerates the elephants. One day, she was feeling particularly punchy and charged at Nyambeni, Shujaa, and Pardamat, all at once. The three elephants bolted back towards their Keepers, surprised by the little rhino's brazenness.

However, there is one elephant who has wormed her way into Raha's heart: Mzinga is our rhino whisperer. The girls have a very unique friendship. When Mzinga comes across Raha in the forest, she abandons her fellow elephants and spends upwards of an hour in the rhino's company.

Developing a territory is very important, as Raha will ultimately be reintegrated into the surrounding Nairobi National Park, which is home to a thriving population of black rhinos. She has already mapped out her forest haunts and confidently leads the way to the next destination at the appointed time, be it the mud bath in the morning or the stockades in the evening, squeaking merrily as she marches along.

Raha is also beginning to exhibit the most famous of black rhino traits: obstinance. One chilly morning, she was all bundled in her colourful blanket and ready for the day — or so we thought. Instead, Raha stood resolutely in the corner of her stable and refused to budge. Two Keepers whistled, but she just stared at them as if they were complete strangers. Compromise was the only solution. They allowed her to remain in her stable with the door

ajar, until she decided it was time to begin the day. Only when she was well and truly ready did she lumber into the trees, like a bright tortoise. Almost exactly one year after Raha was rescued, another tiny miracle entered our midst. On 6th September 2023, a newborn rhino calf was spotted by a waterhole in the free release rhino range of Tsavo West National Park. His mother was nowhere to be found.

Like Raha, much of Chamboi's story remains a mystery. He was even younger than her when he was orphaned — a day old, at the very most — and impossibly small. At the time, Tsavo was at the tail end of a drought and conditions were very challenging. Perhaps his mum intentionally abandoned him, knowing that she would struggle to produce ample milk. It is also very possible that he was born premature, especially given his diminutive size, and was unable to nurse. And of course, with rhinos, it is always possible that his mother got into a fight or was targeted by an amorous male, and the baby was abandoned in the fracas.

Unlike elephants, black rhinos are not social animals. For this reason, orphaned calves are typically raised by their Keepers as an 'only child', mimicking the solitary lives they will lead as adults. Because Chamboi was a rhino of Tsavo, we brought him to our Kaluku Neonate Nursery, which sits in the heart of the Tsavo ecosystem.

Chamboi's arrival marked a 'changing of the guard': Just one week later, Apollo graduated to Rhino Base in Tsavo East. Rescued in 2019, Apollo spent his infancy at Kaluku. Over four years, the squeaking, bobbed nose baby we rescued transformed into a hulking adolescent eager for broader horizons. From Rhino Base, he will continue his reintegration journey and ultimately reclaim his place in the wild.

And thus, completely by chance, the exit of one rhino coincided with the arrival of another. Mercifully, Chamboi did not struggle in the way Raha did, but it was not all smooth sailing with him. He was orphaned at such a young age that he never had his mother's colostrum, which always puts calves on the back foot. For a long time, we battled with a litany of stomach issues. Fortunately, he helped himself by feeding with great enthusiasm. Now that he has his molars and is eating greens, he has become exponentially stronger and more energetic.

While Raha is methodical and unperturbable, Chamboi is more animated and flighty. His preferred gait is a skip — he seems to levitate as he races his Keepers through the bush. (This might be a male rhino trait: Apollo was also prone to bursts of energy, which occasionally necessitated aerial searches to track him down. We will be relieved if Chamboi doesn't adopt this particular pastime!)

Just as rhinos are known for their obstinance, they also love their routines and rituals. Chamboi embodies this trait with fervour. He is obsessed with one specific blanket — a woollen, cherry red number — and flatly refuses to wear anything else. Tsavo can get very hot, but infant rhinos are fragile, much like elephants, and need to be shielded from even the slightest chill in the air.

In February, Chamboi's flock expanded. During a fixed-wing patrol, our pilot was requested to stop in Asa, a remote village northeast of Tsavo East National Park. He returned to base with two unlikely passengers onboard: a pair of ostrich chicks, who had been orphaned as hatchlings. We named them Bam and Boozle.

Bam and Boozle immediately took a shine to Chamboi. He had very little say in the matter; they simply started following him from sunup to sundown! They make an unlikely troupe, the stout rhino and the gangly birds. In typical rhino fashion, Chamboi isn't overly effusive about his 'satellites', as we now call Bam and Boozle, but he certainly accepts their company. They go everywhere together — from the airstrip to the mud bath to the bush and back home again.

Rhinos and elephants are very different creatures to raise. For elephants, family bonds last a lifetime. This includes our orphans, who continue to visit their Keepers long after they have grown up and reclaimed their place in the wild. When rhinos fly the proverbial nest, they do so in a much more definitive manner. This is part of their genetic make-up; they are solitary, serious creatures, and part of growing up means embracing a largely hermetic existence. (But with that said, they also never forget the people who raised them. Just last year, we were treated to a visit from Solio, a black rhino ex-orphan who is now living wild in Nairobi National Park and a mother of two. The fact that this famously private creature felt comfortable bringing her newborn back to the Nursery environs was a telling display of trust.)

As babies, however, rhinos thrive off nurturing care and companionship. Raha and Chamboi, both orphaned as newborns, never really knew their own mothers. Their Keepers are the only family they have ever known. This is immediately clear when you spend time with them: Raha is glued to her Keepers and self-soothes by suckling their trousers; Chamboi's favourite place to sleep is by his Keepers' sides, his eyes closed in bliss as they rub his tummy. Both babies are constantly chattering away with a series of squeaks, communicating through an ancient, delightful, and completely improbable language.

It will be very interesting to see how Raha and Chamboi's journeys unfold, given the uniquely young ages at which they were orphaned. But for now — and for the next several years, at least — these enchanting, ornery, mystifying little creatures will remain very much part of the fold. It is a privilege to play a formative role in their upbringing.

BREATHING NEW LIFE INTO ITHUMBA

— July 2019 —

Since the inception of Tsavo East National Park, Ithumba has been its crown jewel. My father, David, chose it as the park's headquarters in the north during his time as the founding warden of Tsavo East. While very necessary infrastructure was put in place throughout the park, Ithumba and the northern area was deliberately shielded from mankind's incursions so that it could remain a truly wild area.

It remained that way for nearly thirty years. However, in the decades following David's death — when poaching reached its height in Kenya — northern Tsavo was particularly hard hit. With virtually no oversight during those fraught times, illegal activity was rampant and poaching went unchecked. Elephants realised that this area was now rife with threats, and all but abandoned the north. Things began to improve in the late nineties, when poaching was curbed and wildlife numbers began to increase. Elephants, however, remained cautious about venturing further north than the Tiva River. They clearly hadn't forgotten the dark memories of the old days.

In 2004, when we were preparing to establish a new reintegration unit for our orphaned elephants, Ithumba immediately came to mind. The vast, unspoilt wilderness that Ithumba offers simply doesn't exist in Kenya anymore, and we knew that this is where orphaned elephants could hone their wild instincts and ultimately return to a free life. Our top priority was to make sure that this area was the sanctuary befitting the orphans and their wild kin.

So, working in partnership with KWS and with the support of other organisations, we turned to the task of making Ithumba hospitable for both wildlife and the people looking out for them. This was no small task: To secure Ithumba's northern boundary, we installed a 63-kilometre electric fenceline, which continues to be patrolled daily. We also assisted in reestablishing the KWS headquarters in the north, funding necessities like rangers' accommodation, offices and workshops, fuel tanks, water catchment tanks, desalination and the installation of a generator.

Throughout all of this, we wondered — and yes, worried — whether the orphans would have ample contact with wild elephants, given the hesitation herds had about the area. We even mulled over whether we would need to establish mobile stockades along the Tiva River to ensure that these crucial interactions would take place.

Fast forward fifteen years, and today it is hard to imagine that those conversations even took place. Ithumba has morphed into a haven for elephants, with the wild herds secure in the knowledge that this is a place where they are once more protected — and even a place where they can come for help. We watched this all unfold over the years, beginning with the first bold elephant scouts who staked out Ithumba and visited the first orphans there.

Wild bull Rafiki was very much the catalyst for this change. He appeared on the scene shortly after we established Ithumba, and then chose to become a permanent fixture, remaining with the orphans for three months. In fact, he was so comfortable with our presence that he would sleep outside the stockades at night, resting his giant head on a mound beside the gates. He grew familiar with the Keepers, never interfering with them, but carefully observing the orphans and all their routines.

After those initial three months, Rafiki vanished — only to return soon thereafter with a handful of bull sidekicks! They too learned the ropes, disappearing and then reappearing with more and more friends in tow.

That was how it all began. Word spread once the bulls were truly confident that Ithumba was again a safe haven, and slowly but surely, female herds began to converge as well. Over the years, the wild herds and our own herds have become one inextricably linked family, as Benjamin, our Head Keeper in Ithumba, can attest to.

Our old faithfuls return year after year to share the dry season with us, confident in the fact that they will find safe drinking sources and ample food in the area. They have become very attached to the Ithumba orphans and the Keepers, and have fully familiarised themselves with all the routines — so much so that it's often difficult to differentiate between wild elephants and the orphans! Many wild elephants sporting injuries have approached the water trough, so that they might be treated by our team. In recent years, these types of visits have thankfully become less frequent, but it is no coincidence that they know where to come for help.

Trust is at the root of elephants' return to Ithumba. They are safe in the knowledge that we are there to protect them, and we work tirelessly behind the scenes to deliver on this promise: The Trust funds two full time anti-poaching teams in the northern area of Tsavo, complemented by KWS Rangers, and we also have two mobile anti-poaching teams that focus their efforts in the area too during the dry months, when human-wildlife conflict and poaching escalates.

Ithumba is meticulously patrolled by air as well, while our helicopters give us and KWS the unique advantage of being able to place boots on the ground anytime, anywhere. These measures, coupled with our Canine Unit, have made a huge difference to the area — and not just to elephants. Now that the bushmeat trade is no longer unchecked, the buffalo herds on the Tiva River have multiplied tenfold and every other species has flourished in the past decade and a half.

It is a great triumph to see Ithumba transformed into what it is today. Nothing makes me prouder than watching the elephants in action: dependent orphans inquisitively meeting wild friends, bulls lazing in the mud bath, ex-orphans arriving with their families in tow, calves gambolling between the legs of their nannies. At last, Ithumba is back to being the jewel of conservation it was always meant to be.

LUNGS OF KENYA

— January 2023 —

When one conjures up visions of Kenya, the mind travels from sweeping plains to dense bushland. Rarely does a forest come to mind. And yet, it is within these deep roots and sprawling branches that we find the lungs of our country, breathing life into habitats, creatures, and communities.

But our living lungs are at extreme risk. Between 1980 and 2000, Kenya lost nearly 50 percent of its forests. Over the course of just two decades, some 740,000 acres of woodland were destroyed through human activities. This is a trend echoed around the planet: Since 1990, the world has lost about a billion acres of forest. (To put that figure in perspective, that's nearly half the land acreage of the United States.) In recent years, however, rates of deforestation have decreased, which is a hopeful indicator that environmental efforts are successfully taking root.

There is a reason Kenya is synonymous with vast savannahs and bushland. It is a country with relatively low forest cover, with woodlands making up about 5.9 percent of the total national area. However, that doesn't make its forests any less important — that just means every acre counts.

In Kenya, montane forests play an intrinsic role in the health of the entire country. Known as 'water towers', these wooded mountains more than earn their nickname: With their higher elevation, they are uniquely positioned to intercept dense clouds gusting off the Indian Ocean. The water that is trapped in these catchment areas then travels down into rivers and springs that flow across East Africa.

Kenya is dotted with important water towers. The Chyulu Hills, sandwiched between the Tsavo and Amboseli ecosystems, is near and dear to our hearts. This spectacular cloud forest is a lifeforce for southern Kenya, supplying much of the water that feeds our wild-living orphans and the communities who live alongside them. Every day, we see evidence of how this relatively small area allows entire ecosystems to flourish. Tsavo's Mzima Springs, which produces over 100 million litres of crystal clear water each day, supplies water as far as Mombasa. These springs percolate only because of the Chyulu Hills. These rolling forests unfurl above the vast plains and swamps that sit at its feet, reaching far into the heavens and capturing water from the clouds.

In East Africa, water is a treasured resource, largely reserved for the precious few landscapes which are able to capture it. However, Kenya's forests share their wealth. Kenya's five main water towers — the Aberdare Mountains, Mau Forest, Mount Kenya, Mount Elgon, and Cherangani Hills — cover just 2 percent of the country, but they supply more than 75 percent of its renewable surface water.

Historically, we have focused our conservation efforts in the wider Tsavo ecosystem. In recent years, however, we got the opportunity to support Kenya's precious water towers. Fittingly, it began with the highest peak in the country and the second highest peak in the continent. Instantly recognisable for its hulking, craggy outline, Mount Kenya is an icon of the African wilderness. But even a 17,000-foot mountain is no match for human encroachment. In the past several decades, Mount Kenya National Park had effectively become an island, surrounded by dense settlements and agriculture.

Mount Kenya Trust was established to forge a future for the ecosystem, driving conservation and reducing conflict between local communities and the creatures who live alongside them. It spearheaded the Mount Kenya Elephant Corridor, a 14-kilometre elephant migration route that effectively extends the mountain's footprint for wildlife, connecting it to the Ngare Ndare Forest, Borana Ranch, Lewa Wildlife Conservancy, and beyond to Samburu National Reserve. Over 1,000 elephants use the route each year.

Through regular mobile camping patrols, Mount Kenya Trust effectively secures the mountain, elephant corridor, and surrounding areas against pervasive threats. They respond to any emergency calls within the region, tackling poaching issues and illegal activities, while also supporting elephant rescues and veterinary interventions.

However, these teams need proper funding to do their important work. Since 2017, we have supported Mount Kenya Trust and their camping patrols by subsidising the team's equipment, rations, fuel, and logistics. We have also donated two Land Rover Defender 4x4 vehicles to the team, which have taken their daily operations to the next level.

The year after we began working in Mount Kenya, we got the opportunity to support the country's greatest and most threatened water tower. The Mau Forest is the largest forested area in Kenya and its most important water catchment. Located in the heart of the Rift Valley, it fuels the main rivers that provide water to the western region of the country.

Humans depend on the Mau Forest for their survival, but it is human actions that put its very existence at risk. Over the past half century, nearly 37 percent of the forest's original area has disappeared. Many perennial rivers have become seasonal, while clear-cutting of trees has led to soil erosion and flooding. Propelled by steep gradients, eroded soil laden with pollutants and agrochemicals end up in the Mara River, which is the primary water source for countless wildlife and millions of people.

The pressures facing the Mau Forest are many and varied, ranging from land encroachment for settlements to forest degradation through grazing, fires, illegal logging, and poaching. To face these challenges head-on, we teamed up with Mara Elephant Project in 2018 to establish the Mau Anti-Poaching Team. The following year, we deployed a second team in the ecosystem.

These Anti-Poaching Teams exemplify how boots on the ground can transform an unprotected area. Indeed, their impact was immediate. Not only did the team support the arrest of poachers, the seizure of ivory, and the removal of snares and other contraband, but their mere presence acted as a powerful deterrent. One of the most impressive side-effects was the buy-in from surrounding communities. There was a huge turnout for the recruitment for the second Anti-Poaching Team, and we have since trained an outstanding team of rangers. At last, local citizens felt inspired and empowered to help protect the wilderness on their doorstep.

Another key water tower fringes the western side of the Rift Valley. The Aberdares is a hauntingly beautiful landscape, dominated by misty forests and open moorlands. It is known for its trout fishing, but a number of rare and threatened species call the area home, including elephants, black rhinos, leopards, and bongos. Our SWT/KWS Mount Kenya Mobile Veterinary Unit serves the area. Oftentimes, their veterinary operations reflect the wider challenges facing the Aberdares, from human-wildlife conflict to poaching to habitat loss.

Mount Elgon, another of Kenya's main water towers, straddles the border of Kenya and Uganda. Swathed in mist, the volcanic giant is believed to be the oldest extinct volcano in East Africa. Crowned by a massive caldera, the interior of Mount Elgon is honeycombed by a network of caves. Kitum Cave is a favourite haunt of the local elephant population, who use their tusks to excavate salt deposits from the inner walls.

Above ground, however, Mount Elgon is in trouble. With limited local awareness on the importance of preserving the water tower, it has struggled from illegal logging, encroachment, charcoal burning, human-wildlife conflict, and forest fires. The Kenya Wildlife Service deployed a ranger unit to protect the area, but as we have seen time and again, teams must be fully mobile in order to work effectively. To help them reach their full potential, we organised a vehicle donation. In 2022, we proudly handed over the keys to a Toyota Land Cruiser 4x4 vehicle, which will give these rangers the rapid response capabilities they need.

These are but a few examples of our wide-ranging and ever-evolving support in Kenya's forests. In the Shimba Hills, a tree-filled paradise on the coast, our latest large-scale conservation initiative is unfurling. Modelling the conservation management template we successfully deployed in the Kibwezi Forest, we are building human/wildlife-proof fence lines, establishing dedicated Anti-Poaching Teams, empowering community scouts, improving essential infrastructure, and working closely with local communities. We are in the early stages of the same undertaking in the Arabuko Sokoke Forest, another threatened coastal habitat.

But these are stories for another day. For now, we have habitats to protect, wildlife to save, and trees to plant. Through these humble, everyday actions, a much bigger future for Kenya's forests is taking root.

The words of ecologist Aldo Leopold come to mind:, "Let there be a tree — and there will be one."

MURERA'S GIFT

— April 2023 —

"Little hope for recovery."
"It might be kindest to end her suffering."

Paraphrasing, these were common refrains among the vets consulted upon rescuing Murera. We were shocked when the young elephant arrived at the Nursery. Our line of work comes with more than its fair share of tragedy, but seeing Murera's struggle was heartbreaking for even the most seasoned veteran.

The year was 2012, at the peak of Kenya's ivory poaching crisis. Murera began her life as any elephant should, nurtured by her family in the wilds of Meru National Park. That all changed at the tender age of two years old, when she stepped on a poisoned spike trap. A particularly cruel means of poaching, these traps are exactly what they sound like: Poachers embed spikes in a piece of wood, coat the apparatus in a powerful poison, and then bury it on a well-trafficked elephant trail. The victim is physically incapacitated by the trap and further weakened by the poison. After an unimaginably drawn-out demise, poachers are able to track them down and steal their ivory.

However, spike traps are as indiscriminate as they are cruel. This particular trap could have caught anything, but it was little Murera who was unlucky enough to cross its path. The spikes ravaged her feet and left her with deep, badly infected wounds. She must have also taken a serious fall, which damaged her hip and severely debilitated her entire hind end.

I will always remember the afternoon that we rescued Murera. We didn't initially understand the full extent of her injuries — that would come later — but we knew that something was dreadfully wrong. Her little forehead was etched with pain and her body contorted, yet she remained resolutely wild and rebuffed all human help. She clearly knew exactly what species was to blame for her situation.

The day after she arrived at the Nursery, Murera collapsed and had to be put on life support. This gave us the opportunity to conduct a full examination. This was also when many came to the painful, but understandable, conclusion that the kindest course of action would be to euthanise her. This is not a recommendation vets make lightly, but given the gravity of Murera's injuries, it was difficult to imagine she could recover.

My mother, Daphne Sheldrick, recognised that, sometimes, heartbreakingly, being a custodian can mean making the decision to end an animal's suffering. However, in Murera, she saw a glimmer of hope. I recall her saying, as she looked upon the calf's ruined body, "This elephant has a lifespan of upwards of 60 years. Even if healing Murera takes a two-year struggle, it is important we try, as she so wants to live."

Hers was a hard-won miracle. Every orphan requires intensive care, but Murera was on another level. She was too weak to be sedated, which made cleaning her wounds a challenge when she was still wild as could be. Her Keepers remained by her side day and night, slowly building up trust and showing her another side to humans. When she couldn't stand on her own, they formed the scaffolding to help her find the strength. When she stopped eating, they coaxed her appetite back with tiny sips of milk and nibbles of greens. Even when she gave up, they refused to concede and brought her back from death. Murera became the Trust's shared mission: She always had cheerleaders clustered around her stockade, human and elephant, voicing their encouragement and letting her know that she wasn't alone.

My husband Robert had the unenviable task of cleaning Murera's festering and punctured feet. Outfitted with a backpack filled with saline fluids, her injuries were flushed daily and

carefully tended to. The full extent of her hip injury was impossible to ascertain, even with an X-ray apparatus at our disposal. However, it was clearly dire: Murera was unable to remain standing for more than a minute before she was forced to squat on her haunches. For our Keepers, having to witness her contorted body endure so much discomfort, despite our best efforts to elevate her pain, was extremely distressing. We were all guilty of doubting our decision at times, but forced ourselves to focus on the tiny improvements we thought we saw.

One elephant quickly became a sister to Murera. Just ten days before we rescued Murera, another compromised orphan came into our care. Sonje was found with a huge protrusion on her right hind leg, which was likely the result of a fracture that had fused in the wild. It is likely to have been caused by a spear or arrow. While her injuries were by no means as extensive as Murera's, they were serious and also left her permanently lame.

It was heartwarming to witness how these girls drew strength from each other, overcoming staggering odds to find their feet again — in Murera's case, quite literally. She came to us unable to walk, but after a long road and despite her disability, she became the unlikely mini matriarch of the Nursery, universally adored by all.

However, it was clear that we would need to forge a unique path for Murera. She would never thrive in a place like Tsavo, where elephants must often travel great distances. Our two existing Reintegration Units, Voi and Ithumba, sit in the heart of Tsavo East National Park. While Kenya's largest national park is widely recognised as prime elephant country, it would never be a tenable home for Murera, who lacked the mobility required to search for food and water during the dry season. We had similar reservations about Sonje, who would also struggle to cover great distances.

Then a serendipitous opportunity presented itself. The Trust had established a Saving Habitats program in the Kibwezi Forest through a concession agreement with the Kenya Forest Service. This important groundwater forest with its fresh springs flowing into crystal clear pools connects to Chyulu Hills National Park. It was already home to wild elephants who had hit the habitat jackpot: Thanks to its network of underground springs, the Kibwezi Forest has food and water in abundance throughout the year. Protected by our field teams and lush year-round, it provided a wilderness where Sonje and Murera could truly thrive.

And thus, our third Reintegration Unit was born. Umani Springs officially opened its doors in 2014, when Murera and Sonje arrived from the Nursery. While it was founded with their futures in mind, both girls had prodigious responsibilities on their shoulders. Establishing a new orphan unit is an enormous undertaking — it is where generations of orphans will find their independence, reclaim their place in the wild, and start their own families. We rely heavily on the founding matriarchs to propel each Reintegration Unit on the path to success. Voi had Eleanor and later Emily, Ithumba had Yatta, and finally, Umani had Murera and Sonje.

When Murera first stepped foot in the Kibwezi Forest, she was deeply unsettled, as was Sonje. It was the enthusiasm of their friend, Lima Lima, who arrived two days later along with Quanza and Zongoloni to complete the founding herd, who settled them both. Murera excelled as a matriarch, guiding from the rear with Lima Lima assisting up front, so collectively the Umani herd navigated uncharted territory where no orphans had gone before. Murera has always embodied a quiet form of leadership, but even a casual onlooker could tell how she had the absolute confidence of her herd and her Keepers.

However, one particular orphan captured her heart. 'Luggard the Lionheart' graduated to Umani Springs in May 2020. Like Murera, he had been terribly, permanently maimed at the hands of humans; in his case, after a volley of bullets riddled his right hind leg. Perhaps Murera recognised that his injuries mirrored her own, down to the very limb that was compromised.

Murera adored Luggard with a love that was palpable. She put her own reintegration journey on hold to tend to his every need, slowly shepherding him through the forest and standing vigil over him while he napped. He may have not been her son by birth, but he was her child in every sense of the word.

And then, tragedy struck. As the first anniversary of his graduation to Umani Springs approached, Luggard's condition began to rapidly decline. He had always faced an uphill battle to survive, and five years after his accident, his body had simply taken him as far as it could carry him.

Everyone was devastated by the loss of Luggard, but Murera was inconsolable. In the immediate wake of his death, she disappeared for four nights. This was extremely out of character; Murera never strayed far from the dependent herd and always spent the night in her stockade. The Keepers assumed that she wanted to mourn in private, away from the place where she had shared so many memories with little Luggard.

As time passed, however, it became clear that Murera's 'wild safari' had an additional motive. Her belly grew rounder with each passing month and she became increasingly moody. Heartbroken over the loss of her adopted son, Murera decided to go out and find a mate, in order to conceive her own baby. This mission was clearly accomplished during her four-night sojourn, for she never again spent a night away from the stockades.

I will always remember the first time Umani Head Keeper Philip called me, suggesting what we had always thought was impossible: "Angela, I believe that Murera is pregnant." This announcement brought about a mixed bag of emotions. We never thought that Murera's body could withstand the weight of a mating bull. How could she weather a 22-month pregnancy, let alone the not-insignificant process of giving birth?

By then, all we could do was wait, wonder, and try not to worry. All the Keepers rallied around Murera, treating her like a queen even more than they already did. (They all insist they don't have a favourite, but one can't help but notice how they dote upon Murera, or how their eyes light up when they talk about her!) The other orphans seemed to recognise that their matriarch was embarking on a new journey and duly supported her. As she became more easily exhausted, they regulated their pace and curtailed their walks. Mwashoti, Murera's original favourite who is now living wild, took to joining the orphans each morning at dawn, so he might spend the day by his matriarch's side.

Nearly 22 months to the day after she lost Luggard, Murera gave birth to a beautiful baby girl. Despite our concerns, she had a seamless delivery that lasted all of a few minutes. We named her daughter Mwana, which means 'child' in Swahili. It is a most fitting name, for she is the very first child born to one of our Umani orphans — an auspicious occasion that will hopefully lead to entire dynasties of elephants in the Kibwezi Forest.

Murera's journey into motherhood didn't entirely go without incident. While she adored Mwana from the outset, she had a strange aversion to nursing (perhaps wary of how it would distribute weight on her injured leg) and refused to let her daughter breastfeed. Remarkably, however, she allowed the Keepers to milk her, then bottle-feed Mwana by her side. This continued for eleven days and eleven nights, until something finally clicked and she allowed Mwana to nurse from her. From that moment onwards, she has been breastfeeding her daughter like a pro.

As a rule, elephants adore babies. However, it is next level with Mwana. Everyone is simply besotted. Enkesha and Kiasa are jostling for junior nanny duties; Lima Lima, Quanza, and Zongoloni are taking breaks from their wild lives to dote on the little one; Sonje has generously taken over leadership duties of the rest of the herd, so Murera can focus on motherhood; even the boys, who usually can't be bothered about much, are politely curious about the new little cherub in their midst.

And the Keepers! Philip, Adan, Evans, and Sora are absolutely obsessed with our family's new addition. All of them have children of their own — and indeed, they would also count the Umani orphans among their children — but Mwana has become their collective grandchild. They can't hide their pride and adoration and have relished every second of her life. They can, in fact, take credit for her life, for their round-the-clock milking sessions helped save the day. Umani is a place full of precious and unique bonds, all connected by unconditional love.

I firmly believe that Mwana is Luggard's final gift. A twist of fate stole his future, but his memory spurred Murera to embark on a premeditated journey to fill the void that he left. What is so extraordinary is that, up until that day, she had shown little inkling of ever undertaking such a journey. She had never interacted with the wild elephants, preferring to give their boisterous ways a wide berth given her own vulnerabilities. For Murera to launch into the wild for four nights was a departure from all that we had ever known.

As Luggard's time on earth drew to a close, he left Murera with a beautiful child to share life with. I feel sure Daphne and Luggard are smiling down from the great beyond, watching their beloved elephant begin a new chapter with a healthy daughter by her side.

MAKTAO
Born:
20 April 17
TSAVO EAST
NP
LARRO (F)
Born:
March 2018

THE NURSERY'S CAST OF CHARACTERS

— October 2020 —

As the first glimmers of sunlight peek above the horizon, illuminating Nairobi National Park in a golden glow, many of the orphaned elephants are growing restless. Trundling to their feet, each makes a beeline for the elevated bunk in the corner of their nighttime quarters. Reaching up with their tiny trunk, they tug the blanket off their sleeping Keeper and tell them it's time to start the day.

When the orphans get wind of the fact that their neighbours are also awake, lots of rumbling commences. Perhaps they are catching up about the sounds and sights of the previous evening, or plotting for the day ahead. The first order of the day is always the morning milk feeding. Two bottles, still warm from the mixing area, are delivered to each stable and stockade. The babies slurp down their milk in record time, each enjoying a formula tailored to their age and needs.

The youngest orphans are the first to emerge from their stables, checked blankets still swaddled around their round bellies. This is when their older friends grow especially restless, eager to join the fray and coddle their little charges. Once everyone is out of their stockades, they greet each other with great fanfare, as if it has been ages — instead of mere hours — since they were last together. Most mornings, they swing by Maxwell's stockade, tickling the rhino with their trunks as he stands in a stupor or, if everyone is feeling more energetic, racing along the fenceline of his enclosure.

From there, it's time to head out into Nairobi National Park, where the day unfolds organically. Some days, the elephants decide where they want to go; others, the Keepers lead the way, drawing from a number of beats they have memorised. This variety is important. Not only does it keep them stimulated — essential for the well-being of any baby elephant — but it also ensures that they don't over-browse any one area.

The tone of the day often depends upon the season. While we ensure the orphans always have ample nutrition through milk bottles and fresh cut greens, elephants are intrinsically wired this way. During the dry season, the orphans focus their attention on finding ample browse. They spend hours at it, studiously tearing bark off branches or foraging for greens. The wet season, however, is all about play. Surrounded by a buffet of vegetation, they grow delightfully plump, splashing around in mud slicks and sparkling freshwater streams.

Wild encounters always loom large in the orphans' days and, for me, this is the really remarkable thing about the whole setup. While elephants are at the heart of the Nursery, wild herds no longer roam in Nairobi National Park. However, it is home to some of Kenya's most iconic species. Deep within the park, beyond the Nursery herd's patch, hippos bob in the dams and lions stalk across the open plains. Rhinos — a thriving population, including a number of orphans we raised and reintegrated back into the Park — skirt among the bush, many with tiny calves underfoot.

On their daily beat, our orphans come across all sorts of creatures, from towering giraffes to graceful herds of impala. Baby elephants can be quite dramatic, and when these encounters surprise them, hysteria ensues. The Keepers often find the whole herd charging to their sides, trumpeting at the top of their lungs, only to discover that all the fuss was over something as innocuous as a tortoise ambling across their path or a chameleon accidentally dislodged while they reached into the trees.

For more than four decades, the creatures of Nairobi National Park have observed our orphans interacting with their human families. This instils enormous trust among the wild animals. Tree hyrax scurry around the leafy canopies, raising their pudgy babies in the branches above our offices. Birds flit through the stables, stopping for a drink and a dip

in the birdbaths. A coterie of warthogs — who Daphne aptly nicknamed the "ever-hopefuls" — wait expectantly around the canteen. They know we churn out three meals a day and that they can count on a handout of tasty ugali if they get their timing right. White-tailed mongooses, who are also clued into the evening handout situation, duly skulk about. Beyond Daphne's veranda, all sorts of creatures make use of the orphans' mud bath and the waterhole. A buffalo named Helmut and his one-horned sidekick, Horatio, have become a fixture over the years.

By the time the orphans head home for the evening, things are beginning to quiet down at the Nursery. The warthogs have retreated to their burrows, the birds are settled in their roosts, and the Keepers are bunked up in their charges' stables. As the sun sets, a new cast of characters will take centre stage. The air becomes alive with rhinos splashing in the mud bath under the cover of darkness, the distinctive call of the nightjar, even the distant chatter of spotted hyenas.

The orphans themselves are oblivious to this, lulled to sleep by a warm bottle of milk and the muted hooting of the Verreaux's eagle-owl perched on the acacia branches above their stables. Tomorrow will be a new day, full of wild encounters and exciting adventures.

THE BRILLIANCE OF VOI

— July 2020 —

The dry season brings about a beautiful new palette — one synonymous with Tsavo, all smokey greys, peaches, and taupes, punctuated by strokes of brilliant red earth. We have not seen this landscape for a long time, due to this year's extensive rains, but conditions shifted quickly in the past two months. The grasses that had blanketed the landscape in undulating shades of green are now bone-dry, transforming Tsavo into a veritable tinder box.

And as such, another, more jarring shade of red has recently dominated the landscape: the blaze of bushfires. Bushfires are always a harsh reality in a place as seasonally arid as Tsavo, but they have been particularly relentless this year. Already, two swept uncomfortably close to home for our Voi orphans. From Msinga Hill, where our Voi Reintegration Unit sits, one could see smoke billowing ominously on the horizon. Had the fires blazed out of control, they would have destroyed vital feeding ranges, which would have had devastating consequences — not only for the area's wildlife, but also for our own orphans.

Fortunately, our teams are well-versed in firefighting, and working with the KWS, they were able to avert disaster. The fires were contained on the western boundary of Tsavo East, but not before destroying huge swathes of the Irima Plains. That area will not recover until the next rains arrive in November, but crucially, wildlife's key feeding haunts and drinking points were left unscathed.

The dry season is not all drama and devastation. Indeed, as further testament to the resilience of our natural world, there are moments of joy to be found around every corner. We see this every day at our Voi Reintegration Unit, where the orphans have been treated to an increased number of visiting elephants. The wild herds in the area quickly cottoned onto the routine of the Trust's water bowser, which they know religiously tops up the water trough and mud bath each day. Now, the wild elephants hover nearby, waiting to glimpse the bowser making its way over. The moment they spot it rounding the eastern slope of Msinga Hill, they congregate under the wide branches of the delonix tree, patiently waiting for their water deposit.

This is a special time for our orphans. Elephants are a social species, and they relish the opportunity to forge new friendships with wild visitors. All the better if they come with a baby in tow; our girls are visibly delighted by pint-sized visitors and many push their luck in their attempts to get close to them. Some wild mothers are more accommodating than others, but those who are wary of the orphans interacting with their little ones are probably just aware of their kidnapping tendencies! We often see our orphans trying to sneak off with a wild baby, waiting for that precious window of opportunity when the mother and hawk-eyed nannies are momentarily distracted. Of course, their techniques are hardly subtle, and it is never long before the calf is whisked back into their family's care.

We wonder if this behaviour is a symptom of our orphans losing their own families at such an early age, and in their eagerness to start their own families, they try to abduct the babies they find in their midst. More likely, this is more a testament to the whole species' commitment to family, as we frequently witness wild elephants trying to spirit away our orphans. Of course, our ultimate goal is for each of our charges to transition from our care and return to the wild, but this must happen at the right time, when they are no longer milk-dependent and can hold their own against the challenges and threats they will face in Tsavo. We often find that wild friends try to accelerate the process!

This happened earlier this year when Mashariki, one of the girls in our Voi herd, was kidnapped by a visiting herd. It happened unbeknownst to her Keepers, which is quite easy at the moment, given the volume of wild elephants converging at the Voi mud bath. We scoured the landscape, but days stretched into weeks, and she was nowhere to be found. At eight years old, Mashariki could certainly survive in the wild, but orphans usually strike out in the company of fellow orphan friends. And then, just as mysteriously as she vanished, she reappeared. A little more than a month after her disappearing act, Mashariki ambled up to the Voi mud bath with a newfound confidence and spring in her step. While she seemed relieved to be home, she was clearly chuffed by the taste of the wild that she experienced.

It is always interesting to witness how the orphans behave in the presence of wild visitors. Mbegu continues to impress us in this respect. Far from being timid and deferential, as her peers typically are, she has no compunction about asserting her leadership. When she feels that visiting matriarchs are acting overly cocky or forceful around "her" mud bath, little Mbegu takes them on in a matriarch-to-matriarch standoff.

There is one formidable female, easily recognisable because of her distinctive crossing tusks, who is known for her aggressive tendencies. Mbegu must know her reputation, as the orphans and Keepers give her a wide berth, but that didn't stop her from trying to take her on. While Mbegu was ultimately forced to retreat, the fact that she was even willing to stand up to this matriarch demonstrates that our "tiny seed" (Mbegu means "seed" in Swahili) is growing into a force of nature herself.

Tamiyoi is another orphan who is blossoming through these wild interactions. It has not been three months since she graduated from the Nursery, but already she is confident seeking out the company of visiting elephants and happily spends hours in their midst. This is in stark contrast to Tagwa, who made the journey to Voi with Tamiyoi. Despite the fact that she is older, she remains hesitant to fraternise with wild elephants and instead chooses to hover around her human family during these encounters.

As these girls show, every orphan is different and explores elephant society at a pace that works for them. They certainly aren't wanting for opportunities: Many days this month, over 100 elephants came by during the two-hour window of time that the orphans were in the mud bath. Our Keepers have a front row seat to the shenanigans that ensue, and as a result, they are becoming familiar with many of the wild personalities. Crucially, they also witness the important bonds being forged between our Voi orphans and Tsavo's wild herds.

And so, amidst the threat of bushfires and the other challenges wrought by the dry season, we must not lose sight of the miracles happening every day. For it truly is miraculous that these orphans, many of whom have been in our care since they were weeks or even days old, are so seamlessly accepted by their wild counterparts. This is as evident in Mashariki's abduction as it is in Mbegu's standoffs, and even in the more mundane interactions we see around the water trough and mud bath. Tsavo's brilliant red earth serves as the perfect stage for these daily productions, culminating in one momentous achievement: orphaned elephants, who came so close to losing it all, reclaiming their birthright.

BENEVOLENT BULLS

— October 2023 —

Females are revered as the matriarchs, mothers, nannies, and nurturers of elephant society, but one cannot dismiss the roles bulls play. They are the guardians of their species. Often referred to as 'lone rangers', bulls actually lead dynamic social lives. While they don't live in a solid herd structure, they too enjoy and seek out the company of other elephants. Bulls look out for each other and can be touchingly protective of females and babies.

To this point, bulls have played pivotal roles in several of our orphan rescues. Orphans are often shunned from family herds. This is a harsh but necessary truth; baby elephants are very greedy feeders, and mothers would struggle to produce enough milk to sustain both their own offspring and an orphan. However, bulls don't have such priorities at play. While they cannot provide infants with the milk they need to survive, they can provide companionship and protection.

In fact, one of our newest additions, Talek, is alive today thanks in part to a benevolent bull. We're not sure how she lost her family, but she was originally reported trailing tour vehicles in the Mara. As soon as our SWT/KWS Mara Vet Unit wrapped up the hippo treatment they had been attending at the time, they drove to the scene — only to find that the calf had evaporated into the wilderness. We hoped that she had been scooped up by her herd, but she reappeared a few days later, this time walking in the shadow of an enormous bull.

The team proceeded to observe the pair all morning, to be absolutely certain that Talek was indeed an orphan. While he wasn't overly effusive, the bull welcomed his fellow traveller, leading her through plains and luggas on a companionable browsing journey. When the team went in to rescue Talek, the bull continued on his way, perhaps satisfied that his part in Talek's story had come to an end.

Talek's story mirrors another rescue that unfolded almost six years ago to the day. During a routine patrol of the southern sector of Tsavo East, SWT pilot Neville Sheldrick noticed a tiny elephant flanked by two large bulls. He scoured the surrounding parkland, hoping to find her herd, but there were no other elephants in the area. A follow-up helicopter patrol confirmed his findings, or rather, lack thereof.

Tsavo was in the grips of a very intense drought at the time, and one of its victims — an adult female — had been found nearby just a few days earlier. How the orphan came into the bulls' orbit remains a mystery, but they generously allowed her to round out their trio.

Many of you may recognise the subject of this story as Kiasa, who is now thriving at our Umani Springs Reintegration Unit. (Ironically, Kiasa is still flanked by bulls: Kiombo and Maktao, with whom she graduated from the Nursery, are like brothers to her.)

And of course, no story about the benevolence of bulls is complete without mentioning Kandecha. In 2010, my husband, Robert Carr-Hartley, was doing an aerial recce in Tsavo East when he saw a striking bull with perfectly symmetrical ivory that swept to the ground. The following day, our team came across the same tusker, this time in the company of a dozen equally majestic companions. They were surprised to find so many bulls gathered, with nary a female herd in sight.

The reason soon became clear: At the heart of the quorum, dwarfed by his impressive friends, was a yearling calf. He was obviously an orphan, and realising his plight, the bulls had circled round to protect him from predators. Our SWT/KWS Tsavo Mobile Vet Unit trailed the group at a distance for the rest of the day, hoping that the calf's mother might magically reappear to claim her baby. But sadly, that was not to be. Although the youngster looked very relaxed in and amongst the bulls, his body was already starting to show telltale signs of milk deprivation. We consulted with KWS, who greenlit a rescue.

Robert, the vet unit, and six of our most experienced Voi Keepers gathered for the rescue. Although they braced themselves for a complex operation, the bulls didn't show any resistance and dissolved into the wilderness. With their duties relieved, we rescued Kandecha and brought him to the Nursery. Today, he is living wild in Tsavo East, although he continues to visit our Ithumba Reintegration Unit — usually in the company of ex-orphan mums and their young babies. I can't help but think that his first role models would be very proud of the gentle, patient bull he has become.

I could fill the pages of a book with stories of benevolent bulls, but I will close here with a final anecdote that unfolded at Ithumba just recently. In early July 2023, a bull elephant briefly appeared at the stockades. The Keepers immediately noticed that he had an arrow wound in his front right leg joint, but the hour was late and he disappeared into the wilderness before a treatment could be mobilised.

A few days later, to our delight and disbelief, ex-orphans Zurura and Kasigau strolled up to the Ithumba compound with their wild friend in tow. The wild bull proceeded to walk inside one of the stockades for a drink (which is almost unheard-of for a wild elephant), before planting himself outside the compound. He made it abundantly clear that he was asking for help.

An arrow to the joint can have lethal consequences for an elephant, but because our vet unit helped him in time, the bull has made a full recovery. In fact, the team did the treatment right outside the Ithumba stockades. 18-year-old Zurura and 14-year-old Kasigau, who seemed to be close friends with the bull, stood guard throughout. Zurura was particularly attentive, walking right up to the team as they tended to the wound. Once the treatment was complete and the bull was back on his feet, Zurura escorted him back into the wilderness.

We will never truly know what unfolded to bring that bull back into our orbit, but given what I know about elephants, I can surmise: Zurura and Kasigau encountered their friend in the wilds of Tsavo and understood that he was in trouble. Both boys grew up in our care, so they knew exactly where help could be found. That is why they escorted him back to our Ithumba stockades, which they recognise as a place of safety and support.

As these stories remind us, bulls are so much more than the lone rangers of elephant society. They are socially connected and highly sensitive, full of care and compassion. They look after their own — be it a big bull in need of help, or a tiny orphan in need of a family. We can learn a lot from these bulwarks of the natural world.

MOVING MOUNTAINS

— March 2023 —

Moving mountains. In its simplest terms, that is what it means to translocate elephants to safety. Elephants are the world's largest land mammals. Their size is their strength: It is what makes them a keystone species, shaping the ecosystem through their very existence. During the dry season, they dig for water in parched riverbeds, unearthing subterranean springs for creatures great and small. Their well-trod pathways to drinking sources create water catchments in the rains, while their ample bodies form a seal as they wallow, helping waterholes better retain water. Their dung is full of seeds, which fosters the genetic diversity of savanna vegetation. As they move, they open sterile bushland and create room for grasslands, where herbivores thrive. Collectively, their everyday actions drive a healthy ecosystem.

However, an elephant's size can also be their downfall. We live in a world where habitats are disappearing at alarming rates, and elephants feel the effects of development keenly. Freedom of movement is key to the survival of the species. Elephants have prodigious appetites, and during the dry season, they must be constantly on the move in search of adequate browse. Increasingly, their rangelands are dotted with farms, homesteads, highways, trainlines, and entire towns, interrupting age-old migratory paths instilled in them by their forebears.

This creates a significant problem — both for elephants and the people who live alongside them. Elephants are hardwired for survival, just like any other wild animal. Especially during a drought, when resources become scarce, their quest for food and water may take them outside the protection of the park and into neighbouring communities. This even happens when there is ample vegetation on the ground: Like so many creatures, elephants are tempted by the path of least resistance, and the prospect of a farmer's bountiful crop often proves too much to resist.

Human-elephant conflict is a complex issue, with lethal implications for all parties. Many parts of rural Kenya are highly impoverished, with families living hand-to-mouth. Although their motives are purely driven by survival, a marauding band of bulls or even a single elephant can devastate a farmer's crops. When elephants risk a person's life and livelihood, they may be compelled to take drastic measures.

Of course, prevention is the first step. Where possible, electric fencelines are the single most effective way to mitigate human-wildlife conflict, creating a literal border between habitats and communities. Beehive fencelines are a sustainable, non-aggressive way to deter elephants, who have an innate aversion to the buzzing of bees. However, given their upkeep and reliance on water, they are impractical in many arid parts of Kenya. Even electric fencelines are not always a tenable solution — for instance, in an area that borders a river and cannot be fenced in. Occasionally, elephants break through or take advantage of an existing gap in the fence.

That's where a rapid response comes in. Working with the KWS, our Anti-Poaching Teams are the first port of call. They have developed a productive rapport with local communities, who report marauding elephants. They identify the animals from the ground and temporarily remove a section of fenceline, if needed. Sometimes, they are able to push the interlopers back into protected areas using their vehicles, but in most cases, our Aerial Unit provides support.

Pilots must be patient and precise. Despite their herd-based social structure, elephants have a mind of their own — and even the presence of an aircraft is not always enough to shepherd them back onto protected land. Pilots must fly low and slow, firmly coaxing

5000KG

their targets without causing panic. The challenge is magnified when they have a group of disorderly bulls to contend with, as is often the case. These groups can be very large — our pilots have moved as many as 40 bulls off community land at one time.

But sometimes, shepherding elephants isn't an option. There are a myriad of reasons why: the elephant is in an area of dense habitation, or perhaps a road or railway will block their way back into the park. These are mighty stumbling blocks, making safe passage by traditional routes impossible.

And that is when we move mountains.

Human-wildlife conflict has emerged as one of the greatest threats facing elephants today. Conscious that there would only continue to be an increased need for translocations, we made it a priority to enhance our capabilities in this highly specialised area. In 2020, we established our Tsavo Elephant Translocation Unit. This specialised task force is on-call to support KWS in the movement of 'problem' elephants.

Thanks to donor support, we procured a custom-made elephant mover truck. This vehicle, which was created specifically for purpose, was a transformative addition to our fleet. It consists of a wide flatbed with a large crane installed just behind the cab. The power of this truck is almost inconceivable, capable of lifting and transporting a six-ton animal.

The elephant is darted — often from the air — while ground teams converge on the area. The entire success of the operation hinges on this dart. KWS veterinarians are extraordinarily skilled, dosing just enough anaesthetic to keep the elephant unconscious for the duration of the operation.

(A brief aside: You may notice I am referring to the elephant as he. While it is not always the case, bulls are far more likely to be candidates for translocation than females. Females, with their family responsibilities, are inherently more risk-averse than males. With that said, drought drives desperation. In the past year, we have rescued many orphans whose mothers were the victims of human-wildlife conflict — yet another sobering demonstration of the changing ways of the world.)

As soon as the elephant is anaesthetised, the team binds his legs together using custom straps. Then, ever so slowly, the crane lifts him onto the truck bed, where he is secured with a different set of straps. It is slow going as the truck navigates rough roads with precious cargo onboard, but every minute counts. A KWS veterinarian remains by their side throughout, conducting constant wellness checks on the elephant.

Translocations are intense operations, but they are also an example of teamwork at its finest. Everyone knows their role and executes it with perfection. Joseph, our truck driver, plays a pivotal part. He learned to drive with us more than 25 years ago, and now he is the operator of one of the most challenging pieces of equipment in our fleet. It is dangerous, highly specialised work that requires nerves of steel. I have never seen Joseph get stressed, even when he is controlling the crane to deposit a 12,000-pound bull onto his flatbed.

The destination changes for each translocation. However, there are always a few common qualities: Elephants are released deep within the park, in a place where water is readily available. Many people worry that they won't be able to link up with their friends, but elephants have extraordinary methods of communication. Bull society is fluid to begin with; they link up with fellow bachelors for days, weeks, or months at a time, then often splinter off in their own directions, only to reunite later down the road. Simply put, a Tsavo elephant's life is never lonely.

Elephant translocations are a last resort — but they are also a life-saving resort. We have witnessed the lethal consequences of human-wildlife conflict time and again. An elephant who becomes a fixture on community land has a target on their back. Thanks to our ability to move mountains, we can give these creatures a second chance and support the communities who live alongside them.

Unfortunately, I predict the need for translocations will only continue to rise in the future. But when elephants require safe passage, we will be there — by air, by ground, or by crane.

Youjays

HUMPTY, A SPECIAL LITTLE HIPPO

— July 2023 —

Days before Christmas, Humpty splashed into our world. Instead of arriving in a sleigh pulled by reindeer, she was heralded in by a bed of flapping fish, then ferried beneath a helicopter. We weren't prepared to have a little hippo in our midst, nor could we have expected the extent to which she would capture all our hearts.

On 22nd December 2016, I received a call about a tiny orphaned hippo in the Kiunga Forest. This remote woodland sits on Kenya's northern coast, tucked between the ancient port of Lamu and the Somalia border. She cut a lonely figure, bogged in a drying mud hole with only a school's worth of flapping fish for company. Her rescuers waded through knee-deep mud, darted her with a tranquiliser, swaddled her in a wet blanket, and carried her to the waiting helicopter.

There was insufficient space onboard for such a rotund passenger — even an infant hippo carries some serious heft — so Humpty was packaged up and slung beneath the aircraft. The final leg of her journey unfolded within a plane, which delivered her to our Kaluku Field Headquarters. We chose this destination because of the pod of hippos that reside in the nearby Athi River, their throaty calls lighting up the still night.

In our decades of operations, all manner of orphaned wildlife have come into our care — but a hippo was a first! We initially thought we were receiving a male, which Daphne christened 'Humphrey'. Upon arrival, we discovered she was a female, but the name was too perfect to give up. Instead, we modified it to Humphretta (Humpty for short), and thus our little mascot of Kaluku was born.

Humpty's first night with us was very memorable. While we scrambled to create accommodations fit for a hippo, Frans, our Field Operations Manager, volunteered his outside bathroom as a temporary bedroom. Humpty and Frans spent a long, sleepless night together. She was quite frightened and feisty, but Frans refused to leave her side, even as she battered the plumbing and bared her gummy mouth in his direction. By morning, the little hippo was completely obsessed with him.

Of course, Frans already had a full-on job to attend to and couldn't dedicate his entire day to hippo parenting. As we looked for a Keeper for Humpty, a young recruit in the Canine Unit sprung to mind. Joseph clearly had a special way with animals, and we wondered if this would translate from anti-poaching operations to raising orphaned wildlife. Our suspicions were correct, and he proved to be a natural. Humpty adored him from day one.

Meanwhile, Humpty's home was soon complete. On the fringes of Frans's lawn, we built a cosy stable on the shore of a paddling pond. Hippos are known for their love of water, but Humpty's enthusiasm took it to the next level. She immediately slipped beneath the surface and then spent hours bobbing around enthusiastically, cavorting in and out of the water like a stout dolphin. In fact, Humpty's love of water extended into nighttime hours. Joseph kept the door of her stable open, so she could slip out for nocturnal dips on a whim. Returning inside, she would make little noises (which sounded something like "mmm mm mmm") to let him know that it was time for bed.

But sometimes, Humpty's nocturnal wanderings took her even further than her paddling pool. As Joseph recalls, "Sometimes, she would say, 'Let's go to Frans's house!' and take off across the lawn in the middle of the light. She would lounge on the beanbags in his living room, her small head propped up so she could see outside, while I rested nearby on a chair. When she decided the adventure was over, she would take off across the lawn and return to her stable."

RICH
E TRUST

Humpty was very attached to her stable, because she shared it with two special roommates: Sala the lesser kudu and Baba the duiker. Humpty was particularly fond of Sala, who was rescued shortly after her own arrival. They used to troll around the veranda and garden together, touching noses affectionately as they investigated the various plants and flowers.

But mostly, Humpty was attached to Joseph and Frans. When Joseph was home on off, Frans would take over parenting duties. She slept on the floor next to his bed, but only after pulling down a pillow to rest her head upon — Humpty appreciated her creature comforts! Frans recalled one particular night when a leopard was making its distinctive sawing noise outside: "Humpty was very worried about the leopard and could not fall asleep. I reached my hand down, so she could suck on my fingers. Almost immediately, she fell into what I thought was a deep sleep, lying beneath my bed with my hand in her mouth. But how wrong I was! The leopard made a loud noise, and Humpty sprung up with a start, taking the whole bed into the air with her. Needless to say, neither of us slept much that night."

Humpty was an interesting blend of action and relaxation. She loved to explore and quickly mapped out her favourite haunts across Kaluku. The little hippo saw any unlatched door as an open invitation, strolling into bedrooms, kitchens, offices, living areas and the like, and making herself right at home. She often led Joseph on excursions to the nearby pilot's house, where she would scour the living area for cosy areas to enjoy. After testing various cushions on the seats and sofas, she would pull down the fluffiest one and have a short rest.

Hippos have a valve in their throat which automatically shuts to block liquids from getting into their lungs, so bottle feeding was initially quite a challenge. However, Humpty soon got the hang of it and became a very hearty eater. On special days (of which there were many), Humpty was treated to watermelon, which she delightedly chomped through at a blistering pace. She was obsessed with football, although she wasn't above playing dirty: When she tired of the game or thought she was losing, she would simply pick up the ball in her mouth, deflating it and claiming victory in one fell swoop.

Her confidence was off the charts, but Humpty was a very demanding young charge. As Joseph recalls, "I couldn't leave her for even one minute, or else she would start to make her noises. One afternoon, I was getting my lunch while she was napping in the pool. She was resting beneath the water, as hippos do, so I went to quickly fill a plate. But I heard a loud howl, almost like a wolf — Humpty had discovered that I was gone and was very upset with me! She came charging over to the kitchen and remained by me like a shadow."

And then, tragedy struck. As unexpectedly as she arrived, Humpty left us. On the morning of 5th July 2017, Humpty took a mysterious downward turn and died. We were shocked; hours before, she had been cavorting around with her usual joie de vivre. An autopsy revealed that the culprit was a twisted gut, a sudden condition that can claim the lives of creatures big and small. Loss is a heartbreaking but inevitable reality in our line of work, but we were absolutely shattered by her death. Kaluku had lost its mascot.

Humpty was only with us for six months, but she touched all of us so deeply. One of my favourite memories is of my mother sitting in a chair beside Humpty's pool while she cavorted in the water. Daphne was 83 at the time, Humpty just a few months old, but both had such a zest for life.

Daphne left this world the following year. I like to think that Humpty was there to greet her into the great beyond, alongside all the other special souls who were taken before their time.

THE WAITING GAME

— October 2021 —

This time of year, all eyes turn to the heavens. We see the clouds building on the horizon, and all we can do is hope they portend rain on the way — because every hot day takes its toll.

The last two years were ones of abundance. Extraordinary rains swathed the Tsavo landscape in green, proliferating life in all its forms. The old persisted and the young flourished: Babies skirted from every tree branch and bush; every elephant seemed to have a perfectly plump calf following in her wake.

But nature gives and nature takes, especially in Tsavo. Failed rains in April and May created a long, gruelling dry season. Flying over the landscape, we see it unfolding every day. There are parched waterholes, game congregated on rivers, well-trod paths to the few remaining places where water can be found. Creatures are just hanging on, waiting for relief from the skies. This is a pivotal moment: If the rains arrive on time, we will have escaped to the other side. However, with climate change, we cannot take anything for granted. The rhythm of life and predictability of weather patterns are no more. As we wait, we do not know what lies ahead.

Of course, these creatures are no strangers to difficult times. Tsavo has always been a challenging landscape — and the end of any dry season is particularly raw. Tragically, it is elephants who struggle the most. One might wonder why such a formidable creature is the most vulnerable, but this is just another example of how everything in nature has its place. As an apex species, elephants would have few threats to their survival in an ideal world. So, nature has made them fragile: Elephants are greedy feeders with poor digestion, requiring large quantities of vegetation to sustain themselves. Scarcity of food has fatal consequences — and it is the young and old who are the first to fall.

The influx of orphans coming into our care is testament to this fact. Last year, we rescued four elephant calves. In the past two months alone, we have rescued more than twice that amount. Some, such as Taabu and Latika, are direct victims of the drought; others, such as Kerrio and Suguroi, were orphaned by compounding factors.

In the span of a few hours last night, I received calls to rescue three separate orphans whose stories are yet to be told. Many of these calves come to us too far gone, but we approach each rescue with unerring optimism. After all, orphans of droughts gone by, such as Malima, Emoli, and Ukame, were brought back from the brink of death.

In these difficult times, it is quite literally the wisdom of the matriarchs that shepherd families to the other side. The decisions she makes mean the difference between surviving a dry season or succumbing to it — and missteps can have dire consequences. We just saw this with one of our ex-orphans, Makena. As a first-time mother, she did not appreciate how harsh drought conditions were for a newborn. For reasons unknown, Makena whisked her daughter off into the bush for several days and, heartbreakingly, the excursion proved too much for the tiny calf to survive.

Kinna is another ex-orphan who gave birth this month. However, she is armed with years of motherhood experience. We can see how she is making a conscious effort to play it safe with baby Kaia, remaining anchored to water points in order to focus on nourishing both herself and her baby. We know how many compounding factors there are in fostering a vulnerable new life, but we are hopeful for little Kaia's future.

While Tsavo's creatures are fighting for their survival, we are busy defending the territory they call home. Illegal activity escalates during dry seasons, from cattle incursions to arson. Poaching always ramps up, because well-trod paths to waterholes serve as a map for those with nefarious intentions. This also makes work a bit easier for our Anti-Poaching Teams and pilots, as there is so little vegetation to disguise poachers' hideouts, snares, and other activities.

Life may be difficult, but life still prevails. Every day, new babies are being born into this parched landscape. Their first steps may be dusty and difficult, but the winds of change always blow through. Each challenging dry season and generous rain are part of the patchwork of existence here. Collectively, it is the years of stored knowledge that will help these little elephants and other creatures navigate their survival.

For this is what Tsavo is all about. It has never been a gentle place, which is what makes the bountiful previous two years so extraordinary. The signs of rain are there: baobabs in flower, weavers nesting, commiphora sprouting green shoots. Even in the communities, the old sages who have weathered countless dry seasons are predicting rain. While we look to the heavens, we are poised for better times ahead.

WILDLIFE

NIGHTTIME AT KALUKU

— February 2022 —

At Kaluku, we wake up with the rising sun. Its first rays peek over the Yatta Plateau, saturating the compound in its gentle glow. As the day progresses, the giant orange orb makes its westward arc overhead, ultimately coming to rest behind the airstrip. When it is clear, the golden silhouette of Mount Kilimanjaro is the last thing you see before the sky fades to black.

And then, it is time for the day's second act — nighttime.

Nighttime conjures up visions of sleep and stillness. In some ways, that is accurate. The orphans are safely tucked in their stables and stockades, the team is resting for the day ahead, and diurnal animals have found a quiet place to spend the dark hours.

But pause in the still night air, and you will find that the show goes on. Chinks of light shine through the wooden slats in the stable block, inviting you to peek inside. Each bedroom is stocked with bunches of freshly collected greens for the orphans to snack on — in fact, it is often difficult to spot the elephant amidst the jungle! Of course, they also have freshly mixed milk bottles to look forward to, which are fed every three hours, day and night.

Listen closely, and you will hear the sound of music wafting through the air. The Keepers have found that music helps many of the orphans fall asleep. Each stable has its own unique soundtrack: One elephant likes country, another enjoys gospel. The Keepers add to this with their own songs and soothing words.

At Kaluku, the youngest orphans room with a dedicated Keeper. While the Keepers sleep in a bunk bed perched above the orphans (they have to sleep too, after all!), a wiggling trunk often prompts them down to earth. They sit with their little roommate until they fall back asleep, rubbing behind their ears and soothing them with lullabies. Some newly rescued babies really struggle to fall asleep inside a stable. When that is the case, their Keeper drags a mattress out on the lawn, where they rest beneath the open sky. Only once the little elephant has settled into a dreamlike state do they shepherd them back inside, where they sleep soundly for the rest of the night.

Chamboi, the orphaned black rhino, has his own bedtime routine. Rhinos are a particular species, and he is no different. Every night, he must be tucked into his cherry red blanket — no other blanket will do. Unlike Apollo, who perched beneath his mattress like a camper inside a tiny tent, Chamboi prefers to curl up in a certain corner of his stable, where he has a view of the night sky outside.

But the orphans and their Keepers aren't the only ones who are awake. Senior management is on-call day and night. I have always been a light sleeper — and thankfully so! Should there be any emergencies, or even the slightest irregularity in an orphan's condition, I am ready to spring into action.

Over in the Operations Room, the night shift is also burning the midnight oil. As our field presence has continued to grow, so have our hours. SWT/KWS Anti-Poaching Teams often conduct night patrols and ambushes, striking when poachers are most active. While most of our operations take place during the day, it is not uncommon for an orphan rescue or veterinary treatment to extend into the night. For the planned and unplanned, the Operations Rooms is online to monitor teams' movements and respond to any live reports.

And of course, the wild world has its own nighttime rhythm. Kaluku sits in the heart of the Tsavo Triangle, an extension of Kenya's largest national park. The same animals found within Tsavo East National Park also call Kaluku home. On any given day, one might see lions, elephants, buffalos, zebras, kudus, leopards, giraffes, or even wild dogs.

Over the years, we have become somewhat of a sanctuary for Kaluku's resident plains game. As dusk approaches, a zebra family makes their way to the lawn by the staff quarters. They graze for a while, before folding their striped legs beneath them and lying in the grass. Over by the aircraft hangars, a large herd of impala fans out across the airstrip. Calves cavort and kick in the dust, under the watchful eyes of their mothers. Every once in a while, a buck might snort in alarm, but usually it is nothing more than a few waterbucks emerging from the bush to join them.

However, their vigilance is well-placed. Kaluku is very much the wilderness, a place where any creature can roam. Just the other night, a Keeper awoke to light shuffling outside his tent. He looked through the window, only to see a lion making away with one of his sandals!

Even when we can't see them, we know our wild friends are there: Elephants feast in the nearby bush, munching on branches and emitting deep rumbles. Bushbabies spring through the treetops, their saucer eyes shining like a pair of lasers. The guttural call of a leopard cuts across the night air, while genet cats slink towards their quarry. It is one of the most magical experiences, to simply stand still and let this symphony of nighttime life sweep over you.

Before we know it, the nocturnal sounds subside as fingers of sunlight begin to stretch above the Yatta Plateau. The babies stir in their stables, the team laces up their boots and buttons their uniforms. And just like that, another night in Tsavo is put to rest.

GALANA, A CHRONICLE OF MANKIND

— May 2024 —

Landscapes are living chronicles of mankind. In an ideal world, they would be impervious to man — after all, Kenya's wide plains and undulating hills stood long before humans traversed them. But the reality is different. Our landscapes are inextricably linked with our existence.

Galana is a testament to that statement. This sprawling landscape joins with Kulalu Ranch below to form a 2 million acre extension of Tsavo East National Park that sweeps out towards the Indian Ocean. Sharing an unfenced boundary with Tsavo, Galana is essentially a continuation of Kenya's largest national park. It is also an important habitat for Tsavo's wildlife — particularly its elephants. Here, storms blow off the coast and fall in great sheets during the rainy season, which in turn allows vegetation to hold out longer during the dry season.

As nature intended, Galana is a vital artery that supports the beating heart of Tsavo East. But conversely, insecurities in Galana directly affect the national park. When my father, David Sheldrick, was appointed the founding warden of Tsavo in 1948, he looked east, to the vast, vulnerable boundary of the park. This was 75 years ago, when much of Kenya was still truly wild. However, he recognised that Galana, the eastern frontier, could either be an enormous asset for conservation or a liability.

It was during this time that David became acquainted with the Wathas, a Tsavo-area tribe of hunter-gatherers. Their history has always been interwoven with the elephant; indeed, in the legend of one Wathan clan, they are related.

According to the story, a Watha hunter was preparing for a hunt. His wife warned him that if he did not come home with a large animal that had plenty of meat to sustain them, he would feel her wrath. But despite her admonition, he returned with only a small animal (the exact creature varies from storyteller to storyteller). His wife flew into a rage and a deep rumble emanated from her chest. As her anger built, she started throwing her body around their hut and shaking her head side to side. As she did so, giant ears began to grow, her teeth extended into tusks, her nose became a trunk, and she thundered down onto all fours and charged into the bush with a final trumpet. The elephant race had been created.

Years later, the hunter's sons encountered an elephant in the bush. Knowing of their mother's transformation into an elephant, they were reluctant to hunt the creature, although they knew it would provide much food for their family. They consulted their village elders, who concluded that the new species should be treated as a gift. The wife's curse was that she and her elephant offspring had become the very source of food she had demanded. From that day onwards, the Watha became elephant hunters, although they remained reverential of the species and, in their way, respected them as relatives.

For generations, the Watha hunted elephants on a subsistence level. But the explosion of the global ivory trade diverted their ancient practices. The hunters became poachers. With their unparalleled bush skills, intrinsic knowledge of elephant behaviour, and pinpoint accuracy with a bow and arrow, they were lethally effective in this capacity. It is estimated that Galogalo, a prolific Watha poacher who was eventually apprehended during David's time, killed a staggering 2,000 elephants over the course of his career.

Despite the obvious crossroads, David spent a lot of time with the Watha. When we were living in Voi, he passed many evenings in their company, gathered around the campfire and sharing stories. They provided invaluable insight into the mechanics of ivory trade, how ivory went from the poachers to the middlemen to the Arab traders on the coast, and finally to the markets in Asia. The Watha made very important contributions in the development of Tsavo East National Park, helping teams navigate the ancient elephant paths that crisscrossed the wild landscape and then working on the crews that turned these paths into park roads. With their excellent tracking abilities, they also made impressive rangers, although of course they were reluctant to apprehend people from their own community.

And then time moved on. After David left Tsavo, the landscape went through a difficult few decades. Beginning in the 1970s, poaching rose to unprecedented levels. Tsavo's population of some 35,000 elephants dropped to 6,000, while black rhinos all but disappeared. Over time, thanks to concerted conservation efforts, Tsavo East National Park and Tsavo West National Park recovered. But the vast eastern boundary — a place so vital to the security of the parks and their wild denizens – remained a largely lawless land. The collective effect of poaching, charcoal burning, livestock incursions, and sundry other illegal activities degraded the land and created a hostile environment for wildlife.

In May 2021, we were approached to assume management of Galana Wildlife Conservancy, a 60,000-acre area within Galana that is fully annexed for conservation. But it quickly became apparent that in order to truly secure the eastern frontier of the Tsavo ecosystem, we needed to work across Galana and Kulalu Ranches as a whole.

In many ways, it felt like a return to David's early days. Infrastructure was there, but much of it was in severe disrepair. While ivory poaching was largely under control, the commercial bushmeat trade had the landscape in a vice. Bushmeat poachers saw it as open season across the ranches, using snaring and the lethally effective lamping to kill scores of creatures in a single night. This, combined with illegal cattle incursions from the north and extensive charcoal burning, turned Galana into a shell of a habitat.

The indomitable Mark Jenkins spearheaded the work on the ground, until his untimely and shattering passing in December 2022. We knew that the best way to honour Mark's legacy was to continue the work he started. Roads were cleared, airstrips were graded, dams were built, grass was reseeded — no stone was left unturned. We implemented a school lunch program for local students and showed our neighbours that we were there to support them, too (the daring river rescue of a truck driver marooned in the flooded Galana River stands out as a highlight).

Underpinning this infrastructure work was the implementation of an extensive ground and aerial presence. Anti-poaching teams were installed across the landscape, while pilots covered the skies. Our rangers and pilots conducted daily anti-poaching patrols, scouted out illegal activities, and generally sent the message that it was no longer open season on Galana.

And that brings me back to the Watha. Just as David did, we turned to this remarkable tribe to support our conservation work in the landscape they know best. Some of our best anti-poaching rangers come from the Watha tribe. Their ancestors were historic elephant hunters; now, many Watha are using their incredible bush skills to protect their mythological relatives.

Transformation does not happen overnight, but three years into our conservation mandate on Galana, we are already seeing tangible results of our work. It is flourishing into a very healthy environment — and a reminder of the resilience of our natural world. We just protect the landscape; nature does the rest.

I remember how thrilled we were when a single bull buffalo showed up at Lali Camp, our field headquarters in Galana. Now, there are well over a hundred buffalo based there. At first, single elephant sightings were cause for excitement; now, it is easy to lose count during a patrol. Zebras, giraffes, and plains game have also returned to the landscape in prolific numbers, and with more herbivores come more lions, leopards, and other predators, too.

As we enter this new era of conservation on Galana, it gives me such hope to know that the Watha — people whose history is steeped in the landscape, and vice versa — continue to be part of that story. The future of our country's wild spaces is in our hands. I am constantly inspired by the Kenyans who honour their heritage through conservation, using their formidable skills for the protection and preservation of their ancient home.

THE HUMAN-ELEPHANT CONNECTION

— November 2020 —

"We need another and a wiser and perhaps a more mystical concept of animals. Remote from universal nature, and living by complicated artifice, man in civilization surveys the creature through the glass of his knowledge and sees thereby a feather magnified and the whole image in distortion. We patronise them for their incompleteness, for their tragic fate of having taken form so far below ourselves. And therein we err, and greatly err. For the animal shall not be measured by man. In a world older and more complete than ours they move finished and complete, gifted with extensions of the senses we have lost or never attained, living by voices we shall never hear. They are not brethren, they are not underlings; they are other nations, caught with ourselves in the net of life and time, fellow prisoners of the splendour and travail of the earth."

It feels most apt to begin with this quote by Henry Beston, a writer and naturalist whom my mother greatly admired. For one cannot be the family to an elephant unless you appreciate them as equals and in fact understand that they have realms that we can only marvel at. Elephants are complex, emotional creatures. They feel keenly and love deeply. After a lifetime with elephants, I no longer see them as separate species, but as a kindred spirit. I know my mother felt the same, as do the Keepers who raise our orphaned elephants.

Among all the elephants who have touched our lives, Aisha stands out. She came into my parents' care in 1974, when I was just a child. This was before Daphne cracked the code for neonate milk formula. Given that this orphan was just days old, it seemed impossible that she could survive. However, Daphne never backed down from a challenge, saying, "I loved Aisha as my own child, for when one is mother to a little elephant, the commitment must be total and come straight from the heart."

Through Aisha, Daphne found a successful milk formula, one that our orphans have benefited from to this day. She also, at heartbreaking cost, showed us the emotional complexity of elephants. She and Daphne developed an unbreakable bond. When my mother was away in Nairobi for my sister's wedding, despite being well taken care of, Aisha pined for my mother and fell into a deep depression. Her physical condition deteriorated rapidly and she passed away. Daphne's own heart was forever cracked by the loss of Aisha; for the rest of her life, she couldn't speak of this little elephant without welling up with tears.

Every orphan leaves an indelible impact, but there are some who touch your soul and transcend the human-elephant divide. My mother certainly had that relationship with Aisha and also with Olmeg, the first orphan raised at the Nairobi Nursery.

I had a special bond with Ndololo. He was born blind, and had a delightfully crooked tail that reached the ground. He learned how to follow the tapping sound of a cane, and he would join me and my children out in the forest for long excursions. Without sight, his other senses were more acute. He was also very emotionally needy, which of course made me all the more attached to him. Ndololo was with us for three months before he took a turn for the worse. There was not a dry eye at the Nursery when he slipped away before our eyes. The truth is, there have been many orphans who have completely stolen my heart over the years. Thankfully, most of them have flourished; today, many have wild-born babies of their own, forging a free life together with their wild friends.

In the wild, raising elephants is a family affair, and the same applies to our orphans. That is where our Keepers come in, providing the love and support these babies need to thrive. For, just like with humans, elephants' formative years influence the creatures they become as adults. When they grow up feeling loved, they are able to embody those values as adults, nurturing their own families in the same manner.

Also similar to humans, not all elephant emotions are lofty. While they have immense capacity for love, they are equally capable of being petty, jealous, and sometimes even mean. They can hold grudges and have vendettas. This is not a mark against their character, but rather an illustration of just how emotionally complex they are. Sometimes, the babies develop crushes on an individual Keeper. This can quickly escalate into a challenging environment, as they bicker over who gets precious moments with their favourite. Our Keepers are master diplomats, ensuring that every orphan feels special and singled out.

We often say that the orphans select their Keepers. I was reminiscing with Benjamin Kyalo, our Ithumba Head Keeper, about his own recruitment, which took place over two decades ago. As he remembers, "I was nervous, especially when I saw another five individuals there. I wondered how I was going to shine above the rest and paced up and down, waiting for my turn. I was most surprised when I was told to put on a uniform and go out into the bush with the Keepers, elephants, and the other recruits. We were given a month for the elephants to decide which four men out of the six remained. The elephants performed the interview, because they can read your heart."

That is the crux of it. Elephants truly can read your heart — and when you have earned their love, they never forget it. We are reminded of this through the 36 babies our ex-orphans have introduced us to, often mere moments after giving birth to them. Although they are now fully wild, they still choose to share these milestones with the people who raised them. These lifelong family bonds even apply to bulls, who are more independent by nature.

Ndume serves as a poignant reminder of this. In 1989, when he was just two months old, he saw most of his herd killed and narrowly survived being bludgeoned to death. He was frantic and distraught when he arrived at the Nursery, and it took him many months to overcome the trauma he endured at the hands of humans. However, Ndume didn't bear a grudge against all mankind — again, we must marvel at elephants and their generosity of spirit — and grew to embrace his Keepers as family.

Fast forward 26 years, when I received reports of an unusually friendly adult bull who was frequenting a camp along the Voi River. Based on photos, we suspected it might be Ndume, so I arranged for Misheck Nzimbi, who raised him through the Nursery, and Joseph Sauni, who rehabilitated him through our Voi Reintegration Unit, to visit the scene. It had been nearly a decade since Ndume's last visit, so we wondered what would happen. The moment they drove up, the bull raised his magnificent head in their direction. Ndume immediately recognized Misheck and Joseph, and made a beeline for the vehicle, rumbling with delight. It was as happy a reunion as you would see between any long-absent family.

Family is everything to elephants. Love is their north star, guiding and dictating everything they do. We are constantly reminded of this: Mini matriarchs enveloping new rescues in a warm trunk embrace, knowing how scared and vulnerable they must be. Orphans protective of newcomers with disabilities, making daily sacrifices to accommodate their needs. The entire herd bravely forming a wall around their Keepers to protect them from wildlife they encounter in the bush. Ex-orphans proudly striding into the stockades to introduce us to their newborn babies. To earn the love of an elephant is an immense privilege — and it is a true love, one that lasts a lifetime.

SPECIAL THANKS

A big thank you to Sean Michael and George Ngechu for helping me get this project over the line. The spectacular visuals in this publication help bring my stories to life. Thank you to Mia Collis, whose extraordinary photographs can be seen throughout these pages, and to Robert Carr-Hartley, Roan Carr-Hartley, Francisco Grimaldi, and Neville Sheldrick for their powerful photographic contributions.

I would like to thank my family, Robert, Taru, and Roan, for playing such an enormous role in the growth of the Trust. Thank you for your unwavering support and hard work, building upon our conservation legacy.

To the wonderful men and women who work alongside us, day in and day out — often going way beyond the call of duty in the process — thank you for so proudly representing the Sheldrick Wildlife Trust. I know we all feel privileged to play a part in such a meaningful legacy, continuing the pioneering conservation work that David and Daphne Sheldrick began.

To our steadfast supporters around the world, thank you for being with us, through the good times and the bad. Together, we continue our mission to save Kenya's irreplaceable natural world.

Angela Sheldrick

First Edition 2024
Published by Sheldrick Wildlife Trust
Printed by druckpartner on FSC certified paper

ISBN 978-1-3999 -9552-8

www.sheldrickwildlifetrust.org